Build the Rainbow of Your Success

New Edition
Work Smarter, Not Harder with Applied
Wisdom from the East and West

Dr. Robert Lee

Foreword by: Dr. Robert H. Schuller

Copyright © 2014 Dr. Robert Lee
All rights reserved.

ISBN 1479343277
ISBN 13: 9781479343270
Library of Congress Control Number: 2012917675
CreateSpace Independent Publishing Platform
North Charleston, South Carolina

The Buzzing Bee

The story that inspired the writing of this book

When we left the patio door open, a bee flew in. It hit the window repeatedly, trying to get out. We could hear it buzzing as it struggled from the top to the bottom of the window. The bee saw the beauty of the garden outside and worked hard to get there, but we knew its effort was futile.

If it were a fly, we would have used the swatter and ended its misery. However, since the bee is a beneficial insect, we opened the door and chased it out.

At the moment, four important lessons came to mind:

1. Hard work alone may not solve our problems.

2. Often the solutions come from doing it another way by thinking outside the box.

3. Sometimes the Almighty sees us in our predicaments and shows us a way out.

4. Our mission in life is to share any learned lessons with other struggling people and take opportunities to show them a way out.

Two roads diverge in the woods, and I took the one less traveled, and that has made all the difference.
—Robert Frost

Give the world the best you have, and it may not be good enough. Give the world your best anyway.
—Mother Teresa (1910–1997)

Any fool can count the seeds of an apple.
Only God can count the apples from one seed!
—Dr. Robert H. Schuller

Dedication

To all people looking for a bright future,
the new graduates,
the newlyweds,
new Parents,
people looking for meaningful jobs,
people launching new careers,
entrepreneurs starting new projects,
people facing quarter-life or midlife crises,
People depressed about their future, people facing new
health challenges, and to
All the "buzzing bees" in the world!

Words of Life

God grant me the serenity to accept the things I
cannot change, the courage to change the things
I can, and the wisdom to know the difference.
—Serenity Prayer by Reinhold Niebuhr

Knowing others is intelligence; knowing yourself is true
wisdom. Mastering others is strength; mastering yourself is
true power.
—Lao-Tze, Chinese
philosopher and reformer (500 BC)

The road the righteous travel is like the sunrise, getting
brighter and brighter until daylight has come!
—Proverbs 4:18

Science is organized knowledge.
Wisdom is organized life.
—Immanuel Kant, German philosopher

Condemnation (rejection) without investigation is the height
of ignorance.
—Albert Einstein (1879–1955)

Security is mostly a superstition. It does not exist in nature.
Life is either a daring adventure or nothing.
—Helen Keller, author

Zuò fú rén qún **li fāng bǎi shì**
做 福 人 群 流 芳 百 世

Make a contribution to the human race;
leave a sweet fragrance for a hundred generations.
—Chinese Proverb

Foreword

After my many travels throughout the Orient, I've gained a deep respect for the wisdom of the Asian culture. This book is the summary of the author's struggles to find the answers to life's questions. Having been raised in China until his late teens and getting his college and graduate education in the United States, he has gleaned wisdom from both the East and the West that has helped him through life. I believe this book can help people of any age appreciate their God-given opportunities and take steps to fulfill them.

Dr. Lee has been active in our church for more than forty-one years. He served as both a deacon and an elder for many years with distinction.

Dr. Lee came to the United States in his late teens to study to be an aircraft mechanic. He hardly spoke English. When he graduated with honors, he asked one of his teachers about the best engineering school in America. The teacher said that would be MIT, Massachusetts Institute of Technology.

"Well, that's where I'll go!" said the optimistic young lad.

The teacher laughed and said, "Bob, you can't even spell Massachusetts!"

That was true, but it did not stop him. Dr. Lee earned a doctorate with distinction from MIT. His doctoral thesis was among the few chosen to be published by the MIT Press.

Dr. Lee worked many years in the aerospace industry as a space scientist and taught as an engineering professor at the University of California at Irvine. He also had a distinguished career as a businessman and an entrepreneur.

If you can dream it, you can do it! America is truly the land of opportunity.

Dr. Robert H. Schuller
Founding Pastor,
Crystal Cathedral

Contents

Preface		xiii
Introduction		xvii
Chapter 1:	**Red** – Purpose	1
Chapter 2:	**Blue** – Mission	27
Chapter 3:	**Green** – Passion	51
Chapter 4:	**Violet** – Excellent Financial Health	109
Chapter 5:	**Orange** – Our Vibrant Health	131
Chapter 6:	**Yellow** – Our Mental Health	181
Chapter 7:	**Indigo** – Creativity and Applied Wisdom	201
Chapter 8:	**White** – The Ultimate Solution	227
Chapter 9:	Footprints on the Sand	245
Appendix A:	The Amazing Hummingbird	287
Appendix B:	On Stress Management	289
Appendix C:	Marriage Saver	299
Appendix D:	Recommended Reading List	309
Appendix E	Pesticides and Babies	311
Author's Biography		315
***** Five Star Book Reviews *****		317
Index		321

Preface

This book is your "call to action" to build your dreams. It will show you the principles for being your own architect; to design and build your life and your own unique "Rainbow of Success," with wisdom from both the East and West.

Everyone started life like a buzzing bee, hitting the window repeatedly, trying to get to the beauty and richness outside. But we cannot understand why we can't get there while working so hard. Others think that God must have a strange sense of humor. He built a maze for our lives and kept us stuck at the dead ends.

The objective of this book is to show you how you can choose to be a victor instead of being a victim and learn to master your life, reach your maximum potential, and achieve personal success sooner by working **smarter, not harder.**

I will share with you what I've learned through the years, as a space scientist, a professor, an entrepreneur, and a businessman. I will point out the potential pitfalls on the road ahead and help you find the right direction on your adventure through life.

We have but one life to live. How we live our lives, not only matters to us, but also to our families, friends, and our future generations.

In life, some succeed while others fail. Why? Because when the going gets tough, and it will, the tough get going, and the losers quit. The losers always have good excuses, but excuses never lead to success.

Many people blame their pasts. We're all products of the past, but we can choose not to be victims of the past.

Yes, we have a choice! We can take responsibility for our lives or blame others for our failures. We need wisdom and guidance to make our choices positive choices.

> The doors of wisdom are never shut.
> —Ben Franklin

First, we must realize we live in two worlds: the visible (physical), three-dimensional world and the invisible (spiritual), multidimensional world. The physical world is composed of what we experience with our five senses. The invisible world is composed of our knowledge, wisdom, character, integrity, faith, hope, love, fear, worry, greed, frustration, anxiety, peace, spirit, and soul. If God is in it, it goes to infinity!

We design our successes in the (invisible) spiritual world, We build them in the physical world.

You're an unlimited mind housed in a limited body. In fact, the programming in your mind is the common denominator to success or failure.

Our lives are constantly under construction. Success in life is a continuous, multidimensional achievement that can be represented by the <u>seven different colors of the rainbow</u>. These are: purpose (red), mission (blue), passion (green), financial health (violet), physical health (orange), mental development (yellow), and creativity (indigo). I've devoted a chapter to each color to discuss them in more detail.

Interestingly, all the colors come from white light. If we have a well-balanced rainbow, it recombines as white light. (See Chapter 8.)

Our lives are gifts from God. What we do with our lives are our gifts to God. At the end of our lives, we'll present our rainbows to the Almighty. Some rainbows will be bigger than others will be. Unfortunately, some will be a few colors short.

My goal is to help you learn how to work smarter—not harder—and to develop an attitude and a core belief, so you can enjoy the sunshine and learn to dance in the rain.

Science is organized knowledge.
Wisdom is organized life.
—Immanuel Kant

Introduction

An old adage says, "As long as there will be tomorrow, there is hope."

"What is hope? Is there a difference between hope and wishful thinking?"

"I'm just an average person. Can I make a difference?"

"What is truth?"

"What is the meaning of life?"

"What is success?"

People everywhere in the world ask these questions.

This book is the summary of my journey through life to find the answers to these tough questions. I don't claim to be someone great. However, having been raised in China until my late teens and getting my college and graduate education in the United States, I've discovered wisdom from both the East and the West, which has helped to shape my philosophy of self-development. This philosophy has been proven true throughout my professional life as a space scientist, a university professor, and in business leadership and management. I humbly share these findings with you, hoping they will help you.

Your life is a book. You're the author. Depending on where you live, you have an average of between seventy to ninety years to write your "Book of life". This book will have a profound influence on your future and affect the lives you touched in the past and will touch in the future. At present, you have already written the first chapter.

Chapter 1 is your past. Look at your past. Are you happy with it? Are you proud of it? Are there things you regret and wish you could delete? Did you hurt someone? Did you need someone's forgiveness? Did you learn valuable lessons? Did you have real frustrations? Do you wish you had had a mentor or two to help you along the way?

Chapter 2 could be called "Quo Vadis?" - Where are you going?

I leaded in with a Latin phrase to show that this is a commonly asked question since the beginning of civilization. Question: How will you write it? Do you have any ideas?

The last chapter is the answer to three important questions at the end of your life: Did I make a difference? Did I matter? Where am I going now?

The objective of this book is to help you write the last two chapter well, with enthusiasm and delight!

Everyone starts life looking for success. What is success? If you're looking for the financial success of Bill Gates, the fame of George Washington, or the scientific achievements of Albert Einstein, you may be asking for a lifetime of disappointment and frustration. Why? Because you are not Bill Gates, George Washington or Albert Einstein!

You are you, a unique individual.

At the onset, we must realize this basic truth:

Introduction

In a jungle, not only the lions eat!

> Born 19xx
> Died 20xx
> Ate a lot
> Drank too much
> Worked Hard
> Accomplished very little
> Name doesn't matter

Every one of us is unique. True success is to be fruitful and have a happy, fulfilled life that builds on the talents and gifts we were given.

Success is a multidimensional journey in life. It's like building the seven colors of a rainbow. No one can achieve perfection in all areas. It's a perpetual self-development program.

The ultimate objective of this book is to help people avoid the common tragedy of life illustrated to the left.

At first glance, this may look like a cute joke.

Unfortunately, this happens to too many people now. These people aimlessly try to make a living, but never found life. They look for happiness in the "happy hour" and never find it. As a result, they lost their health as well as wealth. Many of these people lock themselves in their own cages, even though the cage door is actually wide open. They never found their purpose, mission, and passion along the way and quit writing their books of life. They die long before they are actually buried.

Have you wondered why two people with similar education, intelligence, and skills differ? Why does one achieve incredible success while the other fails in almost everything he does?

The reason is that they consciously or unconsciously embrace one of the two following creeds:

The Possibility Thinker's Creed

When faced with a mountain, I WILL NOT QUIT!
I will keep on striving until I climb over, find a pass through, tunnel underneath, or simply stay and turn the mountain into a gold mine, w*ith God's help!*
—Dr. Robert H. Schuller

In contrast, there is:

The Impossibility Thinker's Creed

When faced with a molehill, I *'ll quickly make it into a mountain by adding more di*rt So I can QUIT with dignity!

In some top US universities, the graduating class is roughly fifty percent of the entering freshman class. One often wonders why there's such a high failure rate among these specially selected top achievers. The truth is that when the going gets tough, and it will, the tough get going, and the losers quit!

Success or failure is the compounded effect of our daily choices over a lifetime. Purpose, mission, and passion are the foundations for building a rainbow of success. These elements will constantly point to the right directions and help us make the difficult daily choices.

In truth, learning these principles will help you to reprogram your conscious and subconscious mind, build your core beliefs, develop good habits, and take action toward your unique destiny one day at a time.

In other words, you must first develop your inner self before you can achieve what you want on the outside, your destiny.

>What lies behind us and what lies before us are tiny matters,
>Compared to what lies within us.
>—Ralph Waldo Emerson

I hope that the principles presented in this book will help you master your own life that you can write your "Book of Life" with enthusiasm and delight.

>A picture is better than ten thousand words.
>—Chinese Proverb

Throughout this book, many stories from the East and West are shared to illustrate the basic concepts. They're used like word pictures to help you gain a deeper understanding of the truth.

>Ultimately, we'll be remembered for two things:
>The problems we helped solve
>And
>The problems we helped create.
>We have a choice.
>**Choose wisely!**

Chapter 1

Purpose

Why Are You Here?

What You Do in Life Will Echo in Eternity!
You Are Important!

Whether we realize it or not, the things we do have profound consequences in eternity. Some people may think that they are not that important. They are. Here is why.

Everyone knows George Washington, Abraham Lincoln, Isaac Newton, and Albert Einstein were important people. What they did, indeed, echoes in eternity.

Question: Where did they get their knowledge and wisdom? Where did they get their character and integrity? Do you think their parents, grandparents, and teachers had something to do with it?

These people behind those illustrious men may not be famous, but they must have done something right. Passing on wisdom, love, and a firm sense of values to our children and those within our spheres of influence is <u>one of our most important purposes.</u>

Imagine the people who will be part of your sphere of influence. You see your children, nieces, nephews, their children, and their children's children. It goes on and on like a mighty river toward eternity. Would you like to see doctors, lawyers, scientists, and engineers? Perhaps even a president or two?

Here are interesting statistics.

In 1879, there were six family members incarcerated simultaneously. Researchers studied their family tree, going back more than one hundred years. They found Max J., born in 1720, had six daughters and two sons. He and his wife were uneducated alcoholics who had many run-ins with the law. Of their 800 descendants, 310 were homeless, 160 were prostitutes, 180 became drug addicts, and 150 became criminals, including seven accused of murder.

Let's look at another family. Jonathan Edwards was born in 1703. He was a minister and the president of a school that later became Princeton University. He had many children. Among his descendants, thirteen became college presidents, sixty-six became Physicians, sixty-five became professors, seventy-two became judges, one hundred became attorneys, eighty-five became authors, eighty became public servants, three became governors, three became senators, and one was the vice president of the United States.

You're the headwaters of your river. Do you want your river to be clean and bring life to all it touches? Alternatively, do you want it to be polluted so that it poisons as it flows?

We each have a purpose in our lives. It's important to discover that purpose as early as possible.

If you do not have a purpose, it is like you are locking yourself in a prison even though the prison door is wide open, but you have nowhere to go!

Having a firm purpose is the first step toward success!

What Is Your Purpose?

Susan was a forty-year-old widow. Her husband was a top corporate executive killed in a traffic accident. She was left with a huge, beautiful mansion and ten-year-old twin boys, Mark and Tom. The boys constantly fought and argued with each other. After the life insurance money ran out, Susan worked two jobs to pay the mortgage and put food on the table. She was always tired so she had no time for the boys. In short, the boys were raised by the TV, movies, and video games, many of which were violent.

One Sunday, Susan went to church to consult with the pastor concerning her boys' violent behavior.

The pastor said, "We all live in two worlds: the physical and the spiritual. In the physical world, your boys will grow up, develop, and mature with or without you, unless you don't feed them. Men by nature are hunters. They are aggressive, territorial, and fearless. Fighting is natural. As a parent, you must help them develop in the spiritual world. By this, I mean knowledge, wisdom, character, integrity, faith, hope, love, etc. If you don't, they will grow up as savages. Do you know that your TV set is taking over as their parents and building your children's characters and value systems right now?"

"But I love our house and am proud of it," Susan explained.

"However, to keep it, I have to work two jobs. I simply have no time to do anything else. What can I do?"

"Well, success in life is a matter of choices and actions based on your priorities. Your priorities are set by your purpose. I can't help you with that. However, when you go to sleep tonight, commit this problem to God. Maybe He will give you the right answers," the pastor told her.

That night the boys were fighting as usual, and Susan scolded them and struggled to put them to bed. She had to get up early for work.

In the morning, she heard a big commotion and a loud scream. Mark had pushed Tom down the long stairway. She rushed down and saw that Tom's neck was broken. She frantically called 911, but it was too late. Tom was gone.

"Sorry Mom, I didn't mean to…" Mark began crying. "He pushed me, and I just pushed him back. What are they going to do to me now? I don't want to go to jail for murder."

Susan sobbed and didn't know how to answer him.

They could hear the police siren. Mark was so scared and remorseful; he ran up the stairs and jumped off the balcony.

Susan ran after Mark and saw him fall. "Oh, God, no!" she screamed.

Then she awoke from her dream in a cold sweat. Susan decided to stay home that day, make breakfast, and take her precious children to school. She also decided to sell the big mansion and use the money to buy a small condo outright, saving the remaining money for the boys' college fund. Then she only had to work only part-time during school hours to put food on the table and be there when they returned home.

After she shared her plan and the story with the boys, they hugged each other with tears, thanking God together and beginning their journey on the long road to recovery.

Yes, There Is a Purpose for Our Lives

In the famous movie, *It's a Wonderful Life,* the main character, George Bailey, faced a major crisis. He was so discouraged that he wished he had never been born. He jumped off a bridge to kill himself. But an angel, Clarence Odbody, saved him and showed him how wrong he was. For example, if George hadn't been born, he would not have been there to save his brother from drowning. As a consequence, his brother wouldn't have Grown up as a pilot and saved a US ship from being sunk by enemy planes in World War II. Hundreds of lives would have been lost. Only God knows what impact those hundreds of lives have now and would have in the future.

Indeed, if we don't exist, there will be a gap in the river of eternity. How big a gap is up to us.

Parents, help your children discover their purposes early.

As parents, we are closest to our children. At times, you can observe and discover their talents; help your children develop them and discover their purpose early.

When I was a young boy in China, our servants jokingly called me "败家子 **bi jiā zǐ**"— one who will ruin the family's fortune. Why? Because I loved action toys and none of them lasted more than a day or two in my hands. I opened them, trying to discover how they worked. Most of the time, I couldn't put them back together.

My mother knew I had a curious mind and bought more toys for me to work with. She also told the servants to save the toys I had destroyed, knowing someday I would learn to put them back together. She was right! I learned the basic principles of their working parts and later reassembled them all but one.

There was a "putt-putt" boat with no moving parts. You put it in water and lit a fire in the lamp inside the boat. After a while, it went "putt-putt" and moved. I took it apart and couldn't figure how it worked. Oh, that frustrated me! I did not understand the basic principles of how it worked until I studied at the Massachusetts Institute of Technology (MIT) years later and learned about mechanical vibrations and natural frequencies.

When I was in junior high school in Shanghai, I fell in love with model airplanes. I was one of the few kids in Shanghai who could afford to buy a motor. Many of my parents' friends thought I was wasting money again on another expensive toy. My good friends Zhou (周鍾文 Zhōu zhōng wén) and

Hú (胡安宁 Hú ān nng) were also model airplane enthusiasts. Together, we formed a "Model Airplane Club". Surprisingly, after sixty-six years, largely because of Zhou's effort, the club is still going strong in China. It has inspired many young people to go into aviation.

I often wondered what would have happened to me if my mother had spanked me each time I broke a toy.

Parents: please observe and help your children to discover their strengths and find their purposes early.

Don't Be a Dream Killer!

When I graduated with honors from the aircraft mechanic school in California in 1951, I asked an instructor which US school was the best in aeronautical engineering. He told me MIT, Massachusetts Institute of Technology.

As an optimistic lad, I told him that's where I would go. He laughed and said, "Bob, you don't know where it is, and you can't even spell Massachusetts!"

If I had listened to him, I would have missed a golden opportunity, forever regretting my decision and being known as a man who failed because he couldn't spell Massachusetts!

Never discourage a young person with a dream; instead, help and encourage him or her.

The following are stories of young dreamers who found their purposes early.

Bill Gates

Bill Gates's parents always knew Bill had a curious mind. He loved to read, and they supplied him with all the books he wanted.

In his early teens, the mothers from the mother's club at Lakeside, Bill's private school, made an important decision. They raised money in a rummage sale to buy a computer terminal and computer time for the students. With that, Bill wrote his first software program when he was thirteen. It was for playing tic-tac-toe. Bill found his purpose. (Read more about this in "The Road Ahead". Ref. 9 Appendix D)

When Bill Gates was nineteen at the Harvard University, a small company called Intel invented a microchip called the 8008. This company had no software, and only Bill and a few hobby enthusiasts noticed it. The chip couldn't do much, but it could be made to count. Bill wrote a software program for the microchip to count traffic flow. In those days, traffic was counted by cars running over a rubber hose, and the pulses were counted by hand.

Bill started a company called Traf-O-Data. He expected to sell millions of his machines. The machine worked well, but the company failed for the lack of marketing. He didn't know how to sell to the government, his only customer.

Instead of quitting and returning to college, he formed another company named Microsoft (see details in Chapter 3). After a long struggle and lack of funds, Microsoft finally succeeded.

Interestingly, Bill Gates's success didn't come from new inventions, but from a clever bit of marketing, which he learned from his earlier failures. Microsoft bought DOS (Disk Operating System) from a friend, renamed it MS-DOS, and sold it to IBM to be used in its newly developed PC (personal computer). Microsoft Windows was modelled from Apple Computer, which had obtained it as a gift earlier from Xerox.

Twenty years later, by 1995, Microsoft had seventeen thousand employees and did multi-billions per year in business. Bill Gates became the richest man in the world. By staying true to his purpose and not quitting, Bill Gates built a big river of success.

With the success of Microsoft, Bill Gates has created thousands of millionaires and kept tens of thousands of stockholders happy, as well as fed and educated literally millions of children. His multi-billion-dollar foundation makes continuing contributions to improving the education and health of the human race. Bill had discovered his purpose early and went after it with passion. (See more in Chapter 3.)

General "Billy" Mitchell

Because I was fascinated with aviation in my youth, my first American hero was General "Billy" Mitchell. He was widely known as a visionary and an outspoken advocate for developing stronger air power in the United States.

He was a daring, flamboyant, and tireless leader who served in the Army Air Corps during World War I. In 1918, after he led one of the biggest air attacks in Germany with 1,500 planes from the Allied air forces. He was absolutely convinced about the future superiority of air power. He horrified and angered the top generals and admirals by saying that airplanes were the future weapon of choice and could attack cities across the ocean and sink large battleships.

He was ordered to prove his point by bombing some captured German ships. His order was to drop five-hundred to one-thousand-pound bombs at five thousand feet, which the top officials knew was an impossible task with the airplanes of that day. Even when the bombs managed to hit the target, the bomb couldn't do enough damage.

General Mitchell deliberately disobeyed the order and sank the battleship Ostfriesland with two-thousand-pound bombs at one thousand feet. The top generals and admirals were outraged, demoted him to colonel, and sent him to a minor post in Texas.

Colonel Mitchell continued his campaign for an independent air force and an air force academy to train flyers. As many of his best friends and former subordinates continued to die unnecessarily from the fiery coffins (obsolete and poorly maintained airplanes of that day), his criticism of the army's negligence grew stronger. His words fell on deaf ears.

When his good friend in the navy and thirteen of his crew was killed by flying the non-airworthy airship, the Shenandoah, he had to do something drastic. He decided to sacrifice himself and invited his own court-martial by charging the senior army and navy leaders with "almost treasonable administration of the national defense."

At his court-martial in 1923, General Mitchell correctly predicted that in the future, airplanes would fight at one thousand miles per hour in the stratosphere. He warned that airplanes from Japanese carriers would attack the Hawaiian Islands, eighteen years before the actual Pearl Harbor attack!

As expected, he was found guilty and left the army to continue his crusade for the establishment of an independent air force in the United States. He knew deep in his heart that helping his country to have a strong air force was his ultimate purpose and worth his sacrifices.

Many of his ideas were adopted later in World War II by the army air force. The B-25 Mitchell medium bomber was named to honor him.

Unfortunately, he never saw the establishment of the air force as a separate branch of our armed forces. That happened after World War II. He never saw the movie The Court-Martial of General Billy Mitchell, starring Gary Cooper and the many honors later bestowed upon him. However, his vision and self-sacrifice for the love of his country and friends in the service will be long remembered.

General Mitchell was promoted to major general in 1948 and awarded the Congressional Medal of Honor posthumously. An international airport in Milwaukee, Wisconsin, is named after him. Indeed, he was driven by a clear purpose. What he did in life will echo in eternity.

Quo Vadis, Domine?

In the first century AD, the apostle Peter worked in Rome successfully, making many converts. There, the tiny sect known as Christians flourished. In the meantime, Rome's emperor, Nero, burned the old Rome to make room for his newly designed city. Because of the public outcry, he blamed the act of burning Rome on the Christians. Nero arrested thousands of Christians and fed them to the lions.

The apostle Peter fled Rome, confused and fearful of persecution and martyrdom. At the outskirts of Rome, Peter fell to the ground and uttered the words, *"Quo Vadis, Domine?"* (Where are you going, Lord?)

Legend has it that the answer came quickly. "My people needed you. If you do not go back, I will have to go to Rome and be crucified for a second time."

At that point, Peter understood his <u>purpose</u>, rose and returned to Rome, and walked into history.

Note: there is a small church known as Chiesa Del Domine Quo Vadis located about eight hundred meters from St. Sebastian Gate (Porta San Sebastiano) where the Via Ardeatina branches off the Appian Way. It was built to commemorate this event.

You may say, "Bill Gates, General Mitchell, and St. Peter are outstanding people. They're one in a million. What can I do to make a difference?" See what a six-year-old boy did.

Ryan's Well

Perhaps you have heard the true story of a six-year-old boy in Canada named Ryan Hreljac. Ryan came home from school having learned about the lack of clean drinking water in Africa. His little heart bursting, he told his parents that if he could get seventy dollars, he could buy a drill to make a well in Africa. His parents wanted him to learn about earning money and giving and encouraged him to be compassionate. They agreed to pay him two dollars every time he did extra chores. Ryan took to the task enthusiastically, determined to buy a drill in Africa.

Months went by, and Ryan continued washing windows and sweeping the garage. Finally, he raised seventy-five dollars, mostly in coins, which he personally brought to Water Can, an organization working to bring clean water to Africa. The director was moved and told Ryan his money was enough to buy only a hand pump. To drill a well would take two thousand dollars. Ryan was unfazed. "That's okay. I'll do more chores." He went back to work.

The local newspaper heard about Ryan's efforts and published a story about his work. By now, he was seven. Another newspaper and a TV station also ran the story.

Suddenly checks came in from sympathetic readers and viewers.

Ryan kept working. Then the Canadian Development Agency decided to match Ryan's contributions, two dollars to one dollar.

A well in Uganda was built next to a school because Ryan wanted the children to take water home every day. The well has an inscription at its base: "Ryan's Well, Funded by Ryan Hreljac."

Nine years later, Ryan has helped raise more than $1.5 million and built 255 wells in twelve countries, serving over 427,000 people.

If God gives you a purpose, take courage and act on it. Start building your own river to eternity!

A Personal Blessing

When I was six years old, I contracted pneumonia. In the 1930s in rural China, pneumonia was like a cancer. It was almost a death sentence. People told me my mother sat-up all night, holding me while I burned with fever and spat up blood.

I asked my mother, "Will tomorrow come?"

She was crying, feeling helpless and without much hope.

Fortunately, we could borrow a car, and drove several hours to Guangzhou to a mission hospital. There, an American missionary doctor saved my life. (It was believed the doctor may have used an experimental form of penicillin.)

I was too young to remember his name, but I'll always remember and be grateful to the doctor, who had come thousands of miles to give me and countless other children "a new tomorrow."

I often wondered why a rich American doctor would give up his comfortable life and travel to a strange country to save strangers' lives. What is his purpose? What is his payoff? Now, every time I tell this story, I realize that he's being paid! I'm just one of the thousands of kids he saved. He is rich in more ways than money.

A Second Chance (A Personal Lesson)

While I taught at the University of California at Irvine (UCI) in the seventies, one of the courses I taught was "Engineering Mechanics", the first core course in engineering. I had more than three hundred and fifty students in the class. During the final examination, I found that a group of young Asian students (all from a small Asian country) were cheating. I didn't know how they did it, but all their answers were identical and wrong. They even boxed the answers the same way.

I met with the group and offered them three alternatives:

1. I could fail them, and the consequence would be that it would hold up their engineering education for a year. (This course was the prerequisite for all future engineering courses.)

2. I could report it to the dean and higher university authorities, and they would investigate. It could result in some dismissals.

3. I could give them an "Incomplete," and they would have to take another examination after the school break. However, the passing grade would be raised to eighty-five instead of seventy.

They all took the third alternative and passed with flying colors. Many of the students received honors later at graduation.

Yes, I had the power to fail them with a simple stroke of my pen, but that was not my purpose. My purpose was to educate the young. There are many ways to teach them and develop a win–win solution. How this second chance affected each student's future is in God's hands.

Below are several famous Chinese stories that illustrate this point.

Confucius and Arithmetic

Many people from the West mistakenly considered Confucius, who lived 2,500 years ago, as a Chinese religious leader. He was actually a philosopher, similar to Aristotle in the West. His philosophy emphasized personal and governmental morality, correctness of social relationships, justice, and sincerity. He had more than three thousand disciples; most became high government officials.

One of Confucius's disciples was named Tze Lu, an impulsive character who wanted to be a soldier. He always wore a helmet and liked to pick fights. Confucius warned him many times to tone down his temper and impulsiveness.

One day after Tze Lu had learned the "multiplication table", he was very proud of his new knowledge. (Not many knew this "high math" 2,500 years ago.)

A heated argument went on in the silk market. A customer wanted to buy eight feet of silk at three yens each. The merchant wanted twenty-four yens. The customer counted with his fingers and insisted that he had cheated him; it should be twenty-three yens. Tze Lu nosed in and said with authority that three times eight is twenty-four, period!

The argument became so intense, Tze Lu said, "I'll bet my brand-new helmet that I'm right."

The other party was equally upset and said, "I will bet my head that I'm right." They went to Confucius for the final judgment.

After hearing their stories, Confucius smiled and said, "Tze Lu, give him your helmet." Tze Lu was so upset about losing his helmet that he wanted to quit his schooling.

Afterward, Confucius called him in and told him: "Before you leave, I want you to know the difference between knowledge and wisdom. Three times eight is twenty-four, no doubt! But a helmet you can buy again, but no one can buy another head."

The ultimate purpose of knowledge is to benefit the world.
Wisdom is to make sure that it does not cause harm.

Imagine what would have happened if Confucius had judged based on knowledge alone. History would criticize him for taking a life for a one-yen mistake instead of being remembered and respected as the wise sage he was. Did Confucius twist the truth? Three times eight is still twenty four after 2500 years! However, he did save a life.

(Tze Lu did not quit school and learned to become an outstanding official later.)

Note: This story was taught to princes and high officials in ancient China because they have the absolute power of life and death. They must understand the difference between knowledge and wisdom and between justice and mercy. Countless lives may have been saved in the last 2,500 years as a direct consequence of this teaching. In fact, the author may well be one of them. One never knows!

The Archery Contest

Background: Sūn Zi (孙子) was one of the most famous generals in China. Born approximately 2,500 years ago, Sūn Zi is still considered as a foremost military strategist of all time. His book, "The Art of War", has been translated into many languages and was taught in most of the important military academies throughout the world.

Sūn Zi was famous for his unconventional thinking. This is a story about Sūn Zi's education and its impact on the future through common, everyday human actions.

※ ※ ※

One day the teacher, Master Guǐ Gǔ Zi (鬼谷子), decided to test the skills of his students in archery. As they approached the field, one of the students, Peng, quickly spotted a pair of black-and-white birds flying and playing around their nest. Peng downed one bird in flight with a single arrow. Many students applauded, and Peng was obviously pleased with himself. The teacher said nothing and ordered the servants to pick up the dead bird.

Observing the obvious disapproval on the teacher's face, Sūn Zi decided he should choose his target more carefully. Soon his opportunity came. He saw a hawk, diving toward a helpless rabbit that was frozen in fear. Sūn Zi shot the hawk in the midst of its dive. Again, all the students applauded loudly in approval. The teacher said nothing and ordered the servants to pick up the dead hawk.

Later in class, the teacher asked Peng why he had shot that bird.

"Well, it was a small, moving target and perfect for showing off my skill," Peng said proudly.

Purpose

"Peng, do you know that when you kill a bird, you're not just killing a bird? You have wiped out all the future generations of that bird as well," said the teacher. "Sūn Zi, why did you kill the hawk?"

"To save the rabbit," Sūn Zi replied. "You taught us always to defend the weak, and the rabbit was helpless."

"Yes, but you saw only half the picture. In nature, there is an orderly food chain. The hawk's purpose in nature is to keep the rabbit population in check. Observe that even though the hawk has the ability to kill rabbits at will, it doesn't do so. It kills only for food. Nature designed its food chain skillfully so everything is balanced, and nothing is wasted. Man is the only animal that kills for fun," the teacher said. "Sūn Zi, when you killed that hawk, you killed all the future generations of that hawk, too."

"Does this mean that we should eat only rice and vegetables?" the students asked. "Show me a grain of rice," said the teacher. "Do you know that a grain of rice, if left alone and unchecked, has the ability to populate the whole world? Yes, it's a living thing, also."

"Oh, no," the students said. "What else can we eat, if not meat and vegetables? Do we just die?"

"No," the teacher answered. "You can't die because there are many things in your body that are dependent on you for their living. If you die, you deprive them of living also."

"This is a strange lesson. If we can't eat and we can't die, what can we do?" the students asked in total confusion.

"Listen and learn this well. Nature provides us with food in abundance. Everything— animal or vegetation—has a purpose and a right to live. Being on the top of the food chain, people must respect all life. It's perfectly alright to kill for food. However, killing for fun is wanton and wasteful and must be avoided," the teacher told his students.

"Peng, you're ordered to rise early each morning and dig for some worms and feed them to the baby birds in the nest until they are fully grown. Sūn Zi is lucky today because even though he did wrong, his heart was in the right place.

Now, let me ask you a question," the teacher said. "What is your purpose for coming here to learn martial arts, the use of weapons, and military strategy?"

"To kill and defeat our enemies," Peng blurted out. "To make and win wars," said another.

"No! No! No!" the teacher said sternly. "The purpose for all of you being here is to learn to preserve peace. In war, no one wins!

In war, the economy is destroyed. Farms are wasted. Widows and orphans are made, and many often starve to death afterward. So your first duty is to make your country strong, so people can live in peace. Make war only as a last resort. I want to make you generals, not killers.

I have one final surprise for the two of you," the teacher continued, speaking to Peng and Sūn Zi. "Peng will have the tiny bird, and Sūn Zi will have the tough hawk for dinner. I'm sure the two of you will remember this lesson well."

Comment: This story happened almost 2,500 years ago. Even at that time, the Chinese had a basic understanding of ecology. In fact, one of the warlords asked Confucius about the ways to prosperity. "If you do not cut down trees until they are fully grown and do not fish with closed nets, there will be plenty for all," was his answer.

Unfortunately, this teaching was not well accepted because of the large population and human greed.

Historical note: To be historically correct, there were two Sūn Zi responsible for the book Military Strategy, later called "The Art of War" in the West. General Sūn Wu in the Kingdom of Wu first wrote the book. After his passing, the Kingdom of Wu was defeated and left in ruins. The book was lost. Years later, the book was discovered by a scholar and kung fu master, Guǐ Gǔ Zi (鬼谷子), who taught it to Sūn Bung, who happened to be the great-grandson of Sūn Wu. Sūn Bung perfected the book and left it to posterity. The story told here has to do with Sūn Bung.

* * *

The One-Armed Beggar

Background: This story happened in the late Qing Dynasty (1800 AD). In old China, there was no such thing as social security. The people of the same clan lived together in a big house for mutual protection and security. They lived as a group until one person became successful. His first duty was to build a new, big house for his immediate family and his future generations. This story began with the widow of a high government official who had just built a new house.

* * *

"The Yellow River ran over its bank again, Mrs. Wu. Thousands of acres are flooded. Thousands of people are now homeless. We'll soon have thousands of refugees coming our way. Seeing this new house, they'll surely come, begging for food. What will we do?" the servant inquired as he came in with the bad news.

"Quick! Take some money to town to buy more rice before the price goes sky high," Mrs. Wu told the servant.

"We can't buy enough rice to feed those people," answered the servant. "Remember last time. We set up a soup kitchen, and hundreds of people stayed until we ran out of food. We had to starve, too, and still the people cursed us for not caring."

"Don't worry. I have a plan," she said.

When the new house was finished a couple of years earlier, the builder left a load of unused bricks in the front yard. Every time a beggar came and asked for food, she will asked him or her to move the bricks from the front yard to the back yard. When it was finished, the beggar was fed and paid a wage.

One by one, the refugees passed by, refusing the hard work. Many called out an angry curse and some unprintable remarks.

One day a young man came by with a bowed head, bent back, and uncombed hair, begging for food. Mrs. Wu gave him the same proposition.

Purpose

The young man was indignant and cried out, "Lady, can't you see that I have only one arm?"

Without saying a word, Mrs. Wu put one hand behind her back, picked up a couple bricks with the other hand, and started to walk to the back yard.

Perhaps he was embarrassed or hungry. The young man took the job. A few hours later, the job was done. Sweating and exhausted, he sat to rest in the backyard. Mrs. Wu gave him a towel and water to clean up. After that, he was given a nice meal and a silver dollar.

"Thank you, Mrs. Wu," said the young man. "I've never eaten a better meal. You see, when I was begging for food, people gave me their leftovers, and I was ashamed to eat it. Today I earned my first meal. Sorry that your towel is black now. May I keep it as a souvenir?"

"Certainly," Mrs. Wu told him as she watched the young man walk away with his head held high.

This game went on for many days, and the bricks were constantly moving from the front to the back and then back to the front again.

"Why don't you make up your mind, Mom?" asked her young son. "Do you want the bricks in the front or the back?"

"I don't want the bricks anywhere," said Mrs. Wu. "The house is finished, and the bricks are useless as building materials, but they are perfect tools to build men."

"What?" The younger son said, confused.

"Yes. These refugees lost their land, their homes, and many even lost their loved ones," Mrs. Wu said. "They are depressed. They lost dignity and self-respect and want to be fed like pets. I cannot afford to do that. My purpose is to help those who want to help themselves."

Years later, a beautiful carriage drove in front of Mrs. Wu's house. Out stepped a nicely dressed gentleman with a servant carrying a large chest. Behold! The gentleman had only one arm.

"Hello, Mrs. Wu. Do you remember me? I was the young beggar you fed a few years ago," the gentleman said. "I was born and raised in a wealthy home. Because of my handicap, my parents hired two servants to wait on me hand and foot. They changed my clothes, fed me, and even combed my hair. When I lost my parents in the flood, I lost everything. Having only one arm, I felt half a man and useless. I felt like killing myself, but lacked the courage and know-how. When you challenged me, I felt indignant.

However, when I saw you, a small woman, carrying the bricks, I suddenly found myself. When I left your place, my self-pity was gone. I had only one arm, but I had a full brain, and I was educated. I'm not useless.

"I started a small business that grew. Every time I was faced with difficulties, I pulled out the dirty towel you gave me. It reminded me that with blood and sweat, I could overcome anything." The man pointed to the chest. "This contains one thousand silver dollars, a small token to repay you for your kindness."

Mrs. Wu was overwhelmed. "Thank you for your thoughtfulness. What I've done for you is my contribution to society. A gift cannot be repaid. It can only be passed on. Mr. Chu, down the street, is raising money to build a school for the village's children. He could use the help," continued Mrs. Wu. "After all, man's biggest handicap is ignorance. It is not losing your sight, your hearing, your arm, or your legs. With ignorance, you lose your mind, the biggest gift from God."

"You have enlightened me again," said the gentleman. "I will pass on your gift by building the school. Someday these children will grow up and amplify your gift even more."

Food for Thought

When we were born, we were each given unique gifts by a higher power. How these gifts are used will have profound influences in the future. Our purpose is to develop these gifts the best way we can. With a clear purpose, we can look forward to each day with excitement! Without it, we wonder why we have to suffer through each day.

Here is a good metaphor. You are on a sailboat sailing toward your destination. When a storm hits, you sail right through it. Without a destination, however, each wave is a torture, and you wonder why you are out there and want to quit. That's why there is such an alarming rise in suicide rate among young people who do not have a firm purpose, especially among many Asian nations.

Clearly, not everyone can expect to gain the wealth of Bill Gates or the fame of George Washington.

Your purpose is being the best person you can be with the gifts *you're* given and make your rainbow shine for humanity and throughout eternity.

Chapter 2

Mission

Everyone starts life looking for worthwhile occupation: a mission in life. What is it? How can I find it?

We believe that life's mission is to find a way to provide and contribute value to the human race and leave a sweet fragrance for a hundred generations. In Chinese, this is written as:

Zuò fú rén qún **li fāng bǎi shì**
做 福 人 群 流 芳 百 世

Here's another profound statement about life's true mission:

Try not to be a person of success, but try to be a person of value.
—Albert Einstein

Albert Einstein was one of the most influential people of the twentieth century. He was a Nobel Prize winner in his thirties, the father of relativity, and a top contributor in the development of quantum mechanics and atomic physics. This man with uncombed hair, who seemed always to wear the same suit or sweater, hardly looked like an important person. However, he was voted Man of the Century by Time Magazine.

Let me ask a question: What did Elvis Presley, Marilyn Monroe, and Freddie Prinze Jr. has in common? They were successful entertainers, well loved by their audiences, and were financially secure multimillionaires. Yet they all died at a relatively young age, by their own hands by abusing drugs and alcohol. Is this the way you want to be remembered?

How about George Washington and Abraham Lincoln? The first one built a nation and the second preserved the Union. They never gained great riches, yet countless generations born and unborn will be grateful for their sacrifices. Each knew very well that their God-given missions in life were to serve the people. It was worth their sacrifices.

John D. Rockefeller gave away more than $530 million (in 1900 dollars) to various causes. His money helped pay for the creation of the University of Chicago as well as the Rockefeller Institute for Medical Research (later named Rockefeller University) in New York, and the Rockefeller Foundation.

Andrew Carnegie will be remembered for the Carnegie Hall, Carnegie Mellon University, and the many libraries (more than 2,500) he helped build. J. Paul Getty will be remembered for the Getty Museum sitting atop the Los Angeles basin, preserving the fine arts for generations to come. All these gentlemen gave away their worldly fortunes to benefit the world. They all understood the following principle:

> You make a living by what you get; you make a life by what you give!
> —Sir Winston Churchill

In America, society often measures a successful person by his or her net worth, which is tangible. A person of value is measured by his or her significant contributions, based on eternal values, which are often intangible but may reach far beyond his or her own lifetime.

In real life, it's the intangible that manifests itself in everything we do and accomplish.

It's what we are on the inside that determines what we do on the outside. It's the dream that builds the empire. It's the faith that moves mountains. It's our mission in providing value that moves us <u>beyond success into significance</u>.

We Are Blessed To Be a Blessing.

A poor Scottish farmer named Fleming was working on his farm. He heard a cry for help from a nearby bog. He ran to the bog. There, mired to his waist in black muck was a terrified boy, screaming and struggling to free himself. Farmer Fleming saved the lad from what would have been be a slow, terrifying death.

The next day, a fancy carriage pulled up to the Scotsman's home. An elegantly dressed nobleman stepped out and introduced himself as the father of the boy Fleming had saved.

"I want to pay you," said the nobleman. "You saved my son's life."

"No. I can't accept payment for what I did. It's my God-given duty," the Scottish farmer replied, waving away the offer.

At that moment, a young boy came to the door of the family home.

"Is this your son?" the nobleman asked.

"Yes," the farmer replied proudly.

"I'll make you a deal," said the noblemen. "Let me send him to a good school and give him a first-rate education. If the lad is anything like his father, he'll grow up to be a man you can be proud of." And to that, they agreed.

In time, farmer Fleming's son graduated from St. Mary's Hospital Medical School in London and became known as Sir Alexander Fleming, the discoverer of penicillin and winner of the Nobel Prize.

Years afterward, the nobleman's son was stricken with pneumonia.

What saved him? Penicillin!

The nobleman's name was Lord Randolph Churchill. His son's name was Sir Winston Churchill.

Lord Randolph Churchill's purpose was to give a child an education. His generosity, unknowingly, helped develop a Nobel Prize winner, whose invention not only helped save his son's life but countless other lives as well.

Blessings Always Boomerang

Penicillin also saved millions of lives in World War II and beyond. Many living now, including me, owe our very lives—directly or indirectly—to this single act of kindness.

Do you know that everyone of us is indebted to this uneducated and little known Scottish farmer, Fleming?

According to recorded history of World War II, without the strong leadership of Winston Churchill, Britain would have collapsed during the Battle of Britain and surrendered early to Hitler. After Hitler conquered Europe, the United States would have had to fight Germany and the entire group of European nations alone, and we would have had no chance of winning.

Why? Hitler's Germany was well ahead of us in the development of the jet planes, the V-2 rockets, and the atomic bomb. Indeed, without farmer Fleming, all of you may well be speaking German now, and I most likely would be in China speaking Japanese, if I had survived.

A Personal Experience

The Communists took over China in 1949, so my family was forced to escape to Hong Kong (then under British rule) as refugees. I came to the United States in early 1950 in my late teens to study aircraft and engine mechanics.

Many people asked if I had any fear coming to a foreign country, without any relatives or money and cannot speak English well. I can honestly say the "fear" never entered my mind, perhaps because I had a strong mission!

I had three brothers and seven sisters. As the eldest son, I knew it was a big sacrifice for my parents to send me with what was left of their limited resources. My mission was to do well, graduate in one year, get my aircraft and engine mechanic license, and find a job. With the money I earned, I was to bring my brothers and sisters to the United States, one by one, to study and give them a bright future.

Below is a true story about a person whose mission was to help people, including myself, to earn a higher education.

C. T. Loo

Mr. C.T. (Ching-Tsai) Loo was a well-known, wealthy art dealer and a generous giver to Franco-Chinese philanthropies in France in the 1920s. The French government made him a *Chevalier de la d'honneur*, its highest civilian honor.

He came to the United States when the Germans invaded France in World War II. He lived in New York City and worked with the China Institute to help poor Chinese students adjust to their new homes in the United States.

Mr. Loo went to France in 1900 when he was just an idealistic twenty-year-old. He wanted to prepare himself to help reform China. But he had difficulty gaining admission to a French college. Lonely and discouraged, he joined a group of young Chinese Republican revolutionaries, followers of Sun Yat-Sen, (the George Washington of the Republic of China), who had also found refuge in France at that time. Mr. Loo worked hard to raise funds and supplies to support the Chinese revolution to overthrow the Ching Dynasty.

Besides starting a small business in soybean products to make a living, Mr. Loo educated himself to become an expert in Chinese art and antiques.

Surprisingly, his big opportunity came from farms outside Lyon, France, where he found huge supplies of priceless Chinese imperial arts and antiques at a small fraction of their actual worth.

Many in the French army which invaded China and looted the Chinese Imperial Palace and the Chinese capital, Beijing, during the Boxer Rebellion (1898–1901). This army from the Eight-Nation Alliance brought back many Chinese art objects and treasures. To protect these objects from being stolen, they were usually painted black to hide their beautiful colors. Most soldiers did not know the worth of these items, and their descendants knew even less. As a result, these artifacts were literally dumped on estate sales around small farm markets by their children.

Mr. Loo discovered his unique opportunity and started a company to buy and sell the priceless antiques. He expanded his operations throughout Europe and later in America.

"They looted my country, and I looted them back," Mr. Loo often joked.

I read the following story in a Boston newspaper in the 1950s. A couple bought a pair of black, lion-like statuettes from a Vermont farm for five dollars. They used them as bookends. Later, one of the lions fell. A corner chipped and revealed its color green. Curious, the couple cleaned the black paint from the lions and discovered they were made of priceless Chinese imperial jade. They were worth a fortune!

In 1950, Mr. Loo set up the C.T. Loo Educational Fund through the China Institute, which offered C.T. Loo fellowships to outstanding Chinese students struggling financially in graduate school. Though these fellowships were meant for graduate students, they were also, on occasion, awarded to outstanding undergraduates. On a lark, I applied for one at the end of my junior year at MIT.

Later that year, I was involved in a minor auto accident during that summer. As a young student, I did not know how to defend myself in court. The attorney for the other party took every penny from me. I lost my car and was completely broke and would have had to quit school and work as an illegal immigrant.

Fortunately, (I call it a miracle now), I was awarded the C.T. Loo Fellowship, which gave me a new lease on life. (Details in Chapter 9.)

Many other recipients of this fellowship are/were professors and top executives in the industry, all are thankful for his generosity. We would like to follow in his footsteps and give something back. That is why we formed the China International University (CIU). The main purpose is to improve understanding between the East and West and to promote world peace. The motto of this university is "Putting wings in young hearts."

Because of Mr. C. T. Loo's spirit of philanthropy, he believed in his mission of giving back to the world and helping future generations. As a result, he inspired others and is a perfect model for the principle of this chapter.

Pelé

Some years ago, a poor boy was growing up on the streets of Brazil. The boy had a strong leg and kicked everything. He didn't own a soccer ball.

One day, a soccer coach noticed him and gave him a soccer ball. The boy was ecstatic. He found that he could do all kinds of tricks with the ball. He practiced until he could kick the ball, at will, into the small holes of a barrel.

By Christmas, he wanted to give the coach a gift. He had no money, so he decided to dig a hole in the coach's garden for the coach's Christmas tree. The coach asked what he was doing.

When he found out the boy's intentions, the coach of a minor-league soccer team said, "This is the best Christmas gift I've ever received. You can join my team in practice tomorrow."

The boy was so outstanding; he soon became one of the most famous soccer stars at seventeen. He won the World Cup for Brazil over Sweden in 1958. After winning the World Cup three times, he was declared as a national treasure of Brazil. His name is Pelé.

One can never measure the value of a soccer ball that can change the life of one who in turn inspired so many. Yes, Pelé found his purpose; the coach's mission was to give him the opportunity.

A Pair of Shoes

A young man was rushing to catch the train leaving the station. In his haste to catch the train, one of his shoes fell beside the track. Without any hesitation, he removed his other shoe and threw it to his lost shoe.

People asked why he did that.

He said, "One shoe is useless for me. Some poor man will now have the benefit of a nice pair of shoes."

The young man's name was Gandhi, the George Washington of India. He was the great leader who helped India win its independence. Gandhi recognized his mission (in providing value) long before he became a national hero. He understood early in life that his mission was to improve the quality of life for his fellow men and women.

Dr. Robert H. Schuller, Founder of Crystal Cathedral

If you can dream it, you can do it!

The toughest job in the world is to be the President of the United States. He has the responsibility of running the country and tries to do his best. Yet almost 50 percent of the people always disagree with him and criticize his decisions. Some do it because they belong to the other political party. Some do it because of their own agendas, and only a few do it because they have honest differences of opinions.

Mission

The second toughest job, I believe, is that of a pastor of a great church. The pastor is always in the spotlight. If one is a visionary and tries to do something great for God's ministry, one will endure no end of criticism. Some criticisms are from well-meaning friends. Most are from ignorant, small minds, and a few of them actually think their criticisms are doing God a service. Such is the life of the Rev. Dr. Robert H. Schuller.

In 1955, Dr. Schuller came to Orange County, California, to start a church with five hundred dollars, an old car, a small organ in tow, a wife, and two babies. His mission was to build a large church that would influence millions. He could not find any schools or public facilities available to start a church, so he preached on top of a snack bar in a drive-in theater and used the theater as his church. He rang thousands of doorbells and went through numerous difficulties, and God helped him with miracle after miracle.

Ten years later, he secured ten acres of land at the junction of two freeways in Garden Grove, California, and built the Garden Grove Community Church. (See details in Dr. Schuller's first book, Move Ahead with Possibility Thinking.)

In 1970, our family joined the Garden Grove Community Church, now known as the Crystal Cathedral. Having known Dr. Schuller for more than forty years and having served on the church board for many years, I watched him in action against impossible odds. One remarkable aspect I noticed when I first joined the board was that the board chairman's seat was always empty. It was reserved for Jesus Christ. Dr. Schuller always chose to follow his God-given dreams with humility, integrity, and unstoppable energy.

One of his favorite sayings was "God always uses the insignificant to accomplish the impossible." It has inspired millions.

An important incident happened in the mid-seventies. We on the church board had overwhelmingly approved the latest design of the Crystal Cathedral by our architect, Phillip Johnson. The cost estimate to build it was $7 million. We had around $100,000 in the bank, and we decided to move ahead in faith.

At the church board retreat, Dr. Schuller challenged the board to pray for a starting gift of $1 million as a sign of God's will to undertake this big project. We looked at each other, wondering who had a spare million. We all knelt and prayed. Surprisingly, $1 million worth of New York Stock Exchange (NYSE) stocks came from a non-church member. (See John Crean in the next story.)

Eventually the Crystal Cathedral cost more than $20 million to complete. Many criticized Dr. Schuller for wasting so much of God's money. It would have fed so many poor people.

As an aerospace engineer, I was reminded how many people criticized President John F. Kennedy for spending billions to go to the moon. Little did these people know that not a single dollar was left on the moon!

Every dollar was spent on research and development in this country. Most of the advancement in computers, microchips, space science, and the instruments used in medicine to save lives were developed during this period. The knowledge gained will benefit the human race for ages to come.

Critics didn't see President Kennedy's vision and commitment of these billions spent as the tuition fee paid to educate this country toward technological greatness.

Furthermore, from the viewpoint of basic economics, a nation's wealth is not money; it is the circulation of the money. This fund stimulates the increase in productivity, new ideas, new inventions, and new knowledge and businesses that, in turn, increase the circulation of money. It was estimated that each dollar spent in the aerospace industry caused several dollar increases in GNP and a much larger tax base.

For the Crystal Cathedral, all the money was spent feeding the workers and stimulating the economy. The Crystal Cathedral Ministry brought the message of God's salvation and possibility thinking to millions in the United States, Russia, and more than 174 countries.

The church has inspired many discouraged pastors to hang in there and build their own God-given dreams. "Dr. Schuller, you saved my life." These words in letters come from around the world constantly. Dr. Schuller's accomplishments have provided much value to the world and moved him beyond success into significance. (For more details on Dr. Schuller's life, please read his biography, My Journey, (ref. 13, Appendix D, also available in major bookstores and libraries.)

> Great spirits have always found violent opposition from mediocrities. The latter cannot understand it when a man does not thoughtlessly submit to hereditary prejudices but honestly and courageously uses his intelligence.
> —Albert Einstein

Blessed To Be a Blessing

John and Donna Crean had a humble beginning. They started their RV business from their garage and went through many challenges and eventually built and became chairman and founder of Fleetwood Enterprises (a NYSE company).

Their story is shared here not because they made millions, but because their mission was to help others by "giving it back", The John and Donna Crean Foundation has given millions to help many worthy causes.

I first heard of the Creans through their first million-dollar gift in stocks, which kicked off the Crystal Cathedral project. I then had the privilege of meeting this remarkable, humble couple in their Newport Beach home through the Rubber Duckling Race to benefit local charities; also John's "Home on the Range" cooking shows at their home.

An important incident with them happened during the building of the Crystal Cathedral. The project cost was initially estimated at $7 million, a large sum, but one the church board believed manageable. However, because of inflation and high interest rates, the cost has increased to more than $14 million.

"Impossible!" Dr. Schuller said. "This project is not viable."

When Dr. Schuller called John Crean to return his million-dollar gift, John said, "Dig a hole. Bob, it shouldn't cost more than a million to dig a hole for the foundation." Thus encouraged, Dr. Schuller continued and finished this impossible project.

John and Donna Crean contributed a second million-dollar gift to finish the Crean Prayer Tower next to the cathedral. He said at the dedication:

"Discover the joy of giving, and you'll discover the reason for living!"

Mother Teresa (1910-1997)

Mother Teresa is one of the most respected women in Christendom. She was the best example of devotion and personal sacrifice in the world. Many people wonder if her mission in saving the dying in Calcutta, India, was that important. I assure you that it was very important to the people who were dying there.

The following poem is beautifully written and is more beautiful because it was her mission and her life.

Do It Anyway

People are often unreasonable, illogical and self-centered; forgive them anyway.

If you are kind, people may accuse you of selfish, ulterior motives; Be kind anyway.

If you are successful, you will win some false friends and true enemies; succeed anyway.

If you are honest and frank, people may cheat you; be honest anyway.

What you spend years building, someone could destroy overnight; build anyway.

If you find serenity and happiness, they may be jealous; be happy anyway.

The good you do today, people will often forget tomorrow; do good anyway.

Give the world the best you have, and it may never be enough; give the world the best you've got anyway.

You see, in the final analysis, it's between you and God; it was never between you and them anyway.

The reason Mother Teresa was one of the most respected ladies in Christendom is not because of what she said, but because of what she did out of her love for mankind. Her self-sacrifice on behalf of the needy was exemplary. She provided much value to the world. Truly, she was a woman who believed in her mission and pursued it with passion. A more detailed account of her life story is presented in Chapter 3.

A Unique Opportunity

In the seventies, we were attending the Garden Grove Community Church, now called the Crystal Cathedral. A unique opportunity was offered to the congregation: the chance to translate our pastor's (Dr. Robert H. Schuller) book, "Move Ahead with Possibility Thinking", into Mao's script (modern simplified Chinese). The cost was a sizable sum.

I was so enthusiastic that I volunteered to raise the money for the project. I tried hard; I raised only $150 in the short time allowed. I decided to volunteer the money myself—not an easy task on a professor's salary. As this was a nonprofit venture, all earnings from the book sales were to be used to translate other Christian books.

At present, several million copies of the book have been sold throughout China. The proceeds also made it possible to translate many more Christian books into Chinese. Perhaps it even helped obtain the approval of the Chinese government to allow the Hour of Power to be broadcast in Hong Kong.

I tell this story not to claim credit, but because it proves what Dr. Schuller often said:

> Any fool can count the seeds in an apple;
> Only God can count the apples from one seed!

The Secrets of an Abundant Life

Many people think "abundant life" means one must have the net worth of Bill Gates or be famous like George Washington. The question is: Can ordinary people have abundant lives?

In church, I heard the story of: "Two Shovels". It goes like this: "We were given a shovel to move good things out to bless others (our mission) as God move good things in to bless us, and God has a bigger shovel!"

I was impressed with that story and went to the jeweler to have a gold lapel pin made. This pin not only reminds me of the story. Every time I wear it, people ask what the pin is about. It gives me a chance to share the "abundant life" story.

Jesus said: *I've come that* they may have life, and they may have it more abundantly.
—John 10:10

So when your cup runs over, never say, "God, you spilled." Just get a bigger shovel.

The Secret to a Good Marriage: Be a Person of Value

We just celebrated our fifty-seven wedding anniversary. People often ask about our secret to a long marriage. I assure them that it's not because we don't have arguments. In fact, one of my wife's favorite jokes is, "When I married Mr. Right, I didn't know that his first name was Always."

My wife and I are so different that we likely would flunk eHarmony.com tests. In many ways, we're complete opposites. I love to watch football; she hates the noise. She loves to watch cooking shows. I joke about why she watches the show and never cooks the recipes. She counters by saying that I never played football either. We fit more the mode of the Taoist philosophy of yin and yang: two complete opposites who work together to form a perfect whole.

In Chinese philosophy, yin and yang represent the two primal cosmic forces in the universe. Yin (moon) is the receptive, passive, cold, and female force. Yang (sun) is the masculine counterpart, representing force, movement, and heat. The yin and yang symbol represents the idealized harmony of these forces, denoting equilibrium in the universe.

Important observation: Note that for the two parts to fit perfectly together, each one must bend.

Look at our anatomies. Male and female are complete opposites, but when fitted together, they have all the ingredients to make a perfect family and perpetuate our species.

When two intelligent people are living closely together, conflicts will always occur. The secret of a good marriage is in recognizing the differences and committing to work together as a team to provide value to the world, the family, to each other and overshadowing the conflicts.

No man ever grew up looking for a woman he could support for life; no woman looked for someone she could cook for and take care of for life. Each is looking for someone who can provide value so together they make a perfect union and build a perfect family.

Unfortunately, love is blind, but marriage is an eye-opener. Many people soon discover each other's faults and differences. They have different agendas and needs that create conflicts. Instead of communicating and working to resolve them, they wonder if they have made a big mistake. Instead of working harder to provide each other with value and encouragement, they fan the fire of their conflicts and differences. Soon they divorce, using the worn Hollywood phrase of "irreconcilable differences" and create tragic consequences physically and emotionally for themselves and their children.

From a Christian viewpoint, divorce is never encouraged. During an interview with the press, Ruth Graham (wife of the famous Rev. Billy Graham) was asked: "Since she was so different from her husband, has she ever thought about divorce?" Her answer was, jokingly, "Murder, yes. But divorce, never."

In a Christian marriage, the couple forms a triangle with Jesus at the apex and the couple at the base. Any problems can be resolved within this triangle. As God provides value to the couple, so they work hard to provide value to each other. When both succeed in becoming a person of value to the other, the marriage succeeds.

The Secret Code

Two young girls, Mary and Grace, grew up in a happy home. They noticed their parents were always lovey-dovey. Their parents used the same secret code all the time. They used it on their birthday cakes, anniversaries, and even daily. This code appeared often around the house with little notes left on bathroom mirrors, kitchen counters, under pillows, etc. The code was: SHMILY.

Mary looked in the dictionary, but there was no such word. Grace looked online, but could find nothing. The girls asked their parents what it meant, but they smiled and said, "It's a secret."

Years later, the girls' mother passed away. On her gravestone, SHMILY was engraved.

Mary and Grace begged their dad. "Please tell us what the secret code is. We need to know."

The girls' father smiled gently, and with an aged finger, carefully traced SHMILY on their palms. "It means, '**See**

How Much I Love You.' Will you pass it on?" he told his daughters.

Tears welled in their eyes as Mary and Grace realized their parents loved each other and their daughters very much. They had never stopped working to show that love to one another.

"SHMILY. Yes, we'll pass it on. It will be our secret code, too!" they told their father.

Many marriages fail because the couple practiced the wrong secret code: "SHMICY: See How Much I Criticize You." or "SHMICIY: See How Much I Can Improve You."

Little things mean a lot. The little things you do will increase with compounded interest. In time, those little things will build you up or tear you down. Everyone needs to be loved and accepted, warts and all, and everyone needs to love others that way in return. Consider it important in your life's mission to make your marriage work.

Two working together in harmony will always make a better contribution to the world than one working alone.

A couple of useful tools that can help resolve conflicts and create happier marriages are presented in Appendix C.

Star Thrower

After a big storm, an old man ran along the beach, carrying a large bucket. Everyone looked for beautiful, multicolored seashells and driftwood on the shore, but the old man picked up only starfish.

"Why do you choose starfish? Do you eat them?" a passerby asked. "What are they good for?"

"Come and see," the old man said as he walked briskly onto a large rock. He stood and picked up the starfish, one by one, and threw them back into the sea. "You see, these little creatures have no defense against the storm. They were washed onshore and can't get back. They dry up and die. I'm giving them a second chance."

"There are thousands of these little creatures dying on the beach. What difference does saving a few make?" the passerby asked.

"Well, it makes a difference to this one and to this one," the old man answered as he began to toss them back into the sea.

In life, many people are caught in circumstances beyond their control. Our mission is to give them a second chance.

The Ultimate Star Thrower

The historical Jesus is well documented. Whether you believe his deity or not, one must admit he was a remarkable man. His mission was to heal the sick, save lost souls, and give humanity a second chance. For a thirty-three-year-old man who never attended school, and spent only three short years in the ministry, his actions and profound statements have changed the world. Some may say that he must have been a super genius who learned quickly without instructions and had a keen sense of understanding that surpassed all the sages of the time.

If he were such a super genius, would he have chosen to die so young and suffer an agonizing death on the cross? While hanging in agony on the cross, would he have said, "Father, forgive them, for they know not what they do?"

I suggest that, regardless of one's religious beliefs, one must admit that giving one's life to save others is the ultimate star thrower.

How to find your life's mission:

I suggest five tasks to find your life's Mission:

1. Improve what you read. One sure way to become a person of value is to read ten to fifteen pages of a good, positive book daily. A recommended reading list is presented in Appendix D.

2. Improve what you listen to. On your travel and commute, do you listen to constant negative news on the radio? Form a good habit by choosing to listen to good motivational CDs and positive messages.

3. Improve your associations. Who are your friends? Are they positive on the way up or negative on the way down and will drag you with them? You may have to find some new friends.

4. Always look for opportunities to help someone. As you help them, you will improve yourself.

5. Most important, pray for guidance and direction and commit to following them.

Again, these are easy to do and (tragically) easy not to do. If we are consistent and persistent, we'll accomplish our missions and become better people.

We'll become people of value!

Chapter 3

Passion

Vision Accompanied with the Success Triangle Creates PASSION.

1. Vision Makes the Difference

In the first two chapters, we discussed finding your purpose and determining your mission. Now, all you need is vision, which gives you direction.

You see things as they ***are and ask, "Why?"***
But I ***dream of things that never were and say, "Why not?"***
—George Bernard Shaw

The only thing worse than being blind; is having sight, but no vision.
—Helen Keller

> Who is mad (crazy)?
> The man who sees his life as it is,
> or the man who sees his life as it can be?
> —Don Quixote, Man of La Mancha

In the musical Man of La Mancha, Don Quixote asked the above question and then sang "The Impossible Dream". All human achievements begin with an impossible dream. (Go to Google to find the complete lyrics.)

Indeed, all human achievements begin with an "impossible dream." Many try it and abandon it at an early age because they want "triumph without the struggle" and give up believing that it's "impossible!"

Some put actions behind their visions and change the world.

Find a need and fill it,
Find a hurt and heal it,
Find a problem and solve it!

A Great Vision that Impacts A Country—JFK on the Moon Project

On September 12, 1962, at Rice University, Houston, Texas, President John F. Kennedy made this in his famous speech: "We choose to go to the moon. We choose to go to the moon in this decade and do the other things, not because they are easy, but because they are hard, because that goal will serve to organize and measure the best of our energies and skills, because that challenge is one that we are willing to accept, one we are unwilling to postpone and one which we intend to win, and the others, too."

In this speech, Kennedy shared his vision and laid out the reasons we need strong science research programs funded by our federal government and strong science educational achievement in all of our schools.

Many people criticized President Kennedy for spending billions to go to the moon. Little did these people know that not a single dollar was left on the moon!

Every dollar was spent on research and development in this country. Most of the advancements in computers, microchips, space science, and the instruments used in medicine to save lives were developed during this period. The knowledge gained will benefit the human race for ages to come. Yes, his vision did make a big difference! (See also Chapter 2.)

Background: In 1957, the USSR shocked the world with their Sputnik—the first man-made satellite in space. We tried to match that with our Vanguard rocket, which failed. The failure was widely and creatively derided in the press, being called a kaputnik in the Daily Express, a flopnik in the Daily Herald, a puffnik in the Daily Mail and a stayputnik in the News Chronicle. This event greatly embarrassed the United States.

To make matters even worse, the cosmonaut Yuri Gagarin became the first human in space on April 12, 1961. President Kennedy realized that we must refocus our efforts to regain the technological edge to ensure our national security, international leadership, and economic growth.

What is Your Vision?

Many of you may say, "I am just an ordinary person. I do not have the talents of famous people or world leaders. How can my vision make a difference?" Here are some interesting stories that show how the vision has the power to change ordinary lives.

Life at Crossroads

A girl with uncombed hair cried bitterly on a bridge. She looked like she had been crying a long time and was suffering greatly inside. She finally found the courage to climb the railing and jumped into the river.

As she struggled for her last breath, an old fisherman pulled her out and saved her life. As they dried themselves, she told her story:

"My name is Mary. I'm a twenty-two-year-old college student. When I entered college two years ago for nurse's training, my parents were so proud of me. They hugged me repeatedly and reluctantly let me leave. I was young, bright, attractive, and full of life. I looked forward to each day with excitement.

"Then I met Fred, a charming, good-looking man who was bigger than life. He has shown me worlds I had never seen. We were instantly in love. I didn't know he was a drug addict.

"In his company, I learned to drink and take drugs. Life was beautiful until I took Fred to meet my parents. After taking one look at Fred, my parents knew he was bad for me. They forbade the relationship. However, we were too much in love to care, so I moved out of the dorm and in with Fred.

"A few months later, I was pregnant. We were still happy together until the baby was born with severe health defects and drug dependency. In the hospital, they didn't allow me to feed the baby until I had undergone a drug detoxification program. Fred left me and blamed me for being stupid and ruining our lives by having the sick baby.

"After a short struggle in the hospital, the baby died. I had no money to pay the hospital and has no place to go. I was too ashamed to return home and too proud to beg. Selling my body would be worse than death. Jumping into the river was the only solution."

"You are wrong, my child," the old fisherman told her. "You are focusing on the past and are blind to your future. Let's look at your assets. You are twenty-two and beautiful. There are literally millions of wonderful young men looking eagerly for you. You can choose good or evil. Most important, you can choose to <u>waste or to invest</u> your life!

"In the last two years, you have wasted your life. Now you have a second chance to invest it," the old man said. "I want you to close your eyes and see the vision of your future. First, you go home to ask your parents' forgiveness. They will welcome you with open arms and tears of joy. You will heal three broken hearts at once. They will help you finish your detoxification program and school. Now, see yourself graduating with your nursing degree. Marry a fine, young man, and raise a big, happy family. Can you see your kids, grandkids, and great-grandkids going onward to eternity?"

"Yes, yes, I can see it now. Thank you!" Mary answered.

When she came out of her trance, the old man was gone. "Thank you, God, for giving me a second chance," she said as she burst out crying. This time her tears were full of joy instead of sadness.

She was still young, bright, beautiful, and vibrant. There was much to look forward to. Thank you, God! Furthermore, she was happily going home.

Note: Her circumstances hadn't changed a bit in the last few hours, but her life had changed. Her vision for her future had changed. **She was looking forward instead of backward.** She won the battle of her mind and was on the path to winning her invisible war, one step at a time.

A Night Janitor

An Asian night janitor was happily singing while cleaning the latrine. Most people considered this a meaningless, dead-end job.

"Why are you so happy, Joe?" a passerby asked.

"This is my second job," Joe answered in his broken English.

"My first job supports my family. Every dollar from this job goes to my son's medical school fund. You see, I'm happy not for cleaning the toilets, but because I'm building a doctor."

With that in mind, do you think he is a success? "He is just a janitor," you may say. Look again. He has purpose, mission, and vision. He loves his family and is enjoying life, working hard to build his legacy.

Do you think his son will ever quit medical school? He would die first. Do you think his future offspring will be janitors? With each stroke of his mop, he follows his vision and builds a bright future for his family.

Setting Goals and Making Commitments

> If there is no vision of the future,
> there is no power in the present.

A good adage says, "A Ferrari never wins any races while sitting in the garage." The greatest waste is unfulfilled potential.

Success is the progressive realization of your vision and dreams. Once vision gets you started, you must stretch your mind and make firm commitments. You must set your goals and plan your actions. Goals are visions with a deadline; they give you direction, but actions get you there.

For example, it's easy for a teenage girl to say she wants to be a doctor. To do so, she must set goals, make plans, and take action. She must decide to improve her grades, determine the college to attend, find the entrance requirements, and prepare for them. Yes, it costs a lot to go to medical school. Can her parents afford it? If not, there are scholarships, fellowships, and student loans. Find the knowledge one needs and apply it. If there is a will, there is a way!

> Know your end point (goal),
> the object of your pursuit then determined.
> That being determined, a calm tranquility may be attained.
> With tranquility, comes peace.
> With peace, you may enter into careful deliberation and planning.
> It is with careful deliberation and planning
> that one attains the desired goal.
> —Confucius, The Great Learning (500 BC)

> Begin with the end point in mind.
> —Stephen Covey, author

> If you fail to plan, you are planning to fail!
> —Benjamin Franklin

The Success Triangle

Success is a journey and an adventure, not a destination.

The journey of a thousand miles begins with a single step.
—A Chinese Proverb

If you want success, you need to have a vision for where you want to go, make your plans, and start the journey by putting one foot in front of the other.

In an excellent book called "The Slight Edge" (Ref.8 Appendix D), author Jeff Olson points out that things pertaining to success are often "easy to do and also easy not to do!" For example, we know exercise is good for health. Yet, if we do the exercise today, we do not necessarily feel healthier right away. If we do not exercise today, it does not mean we get noticeably weaker. The health benefit will come if we are consistent and persistent.

Mr. Olson wrote that "success is a progressive realization of a worthwhile ideal." It is never a quantum leap. Success is the compounded effect of our daily activities, one baby step at a time.

He told a profound story about a millionaire on his deathbed. The millionaire gave his two sons a choice: they could have a million dollars or one penny that doubled every day for thirty days.

Most people would jump for the one million. However, if one chooses the latter, he will have more than $5.8 million dollars in thirty days! This is the power of compound interest!

Mr. Olson's theme was to achieve success not with a quantum leap, but by starting small and being consistent and persistent by taking action with one small step at a time. The compound effect will get you anywhere you want to go. I highly recommend this book.

> One of the greatest inventions in
> human history is
> "compound interest."
> —Albert Einstein

A Stupid Game

A twelve-year-old boy sat in the street doing nothing.

An old gentleman came by and asked if the boy had ever played baseball. The answer was no.

"Come with me to the park," the old man said. "I'll throw the ball to you. All you have to do is hit it with this bat."

"I can do that. It's easy," the boy said enthusiastically.

"Okay. Let's begin. Here is the first ball," the man told him at the park.

The boy swung with all his might and missed. He swung and missed again. Ten balls and ten misses later, the boy threw down the bat and said, "I don't like this. It's a stupid game."

"All you need is practice and training. Keep trying and you will get better at it," the old man said as he left.

The next day the boy went to the park and tried and missed again. He even took advice from others in the park. He found that he did improve a bit, but then if he hit the ball, someone always caught it.

Years later, the old man spotted the boy sitting on the street. "How's your baseball career doing?" asked the old man.

"I gave up. It's just a stupid game. I've better things to do," was the reply. "Well, I knew someone who managed to hit only three balls out of ten (a batting average of three hundred)," said the old man. "This stupid game pays him four million dollars a year. What are you making now?"

Belief, Focus, Activity, Integrity

If you are looking for success in any area, here are four basic factors to consider:

1. Belief: Once we have the vision to do something, our belief systems often weaken as time passes. We must reaffirm and strengthen it constantly.
2. Focus: Life is full of distractions. If we don't focus on our goals, we become a wandering generality, going nowhere.
3. Activity: "The journey of a thousand miles begins with a single step!" Once you start, keep putting one foot in front of the other and continue. If you want to get to your destination, quitting is never an option.
4. Integrity: Integrity is what you do when no one is looking. It's keeping a promise between yourself and

God, no matter what happens. For example, recently, we exited a store after shopping. Upon loading the bags to the car, we found a small item left in the cart unnoticed by the clerk or us. The item cost only $4.95. My first impulse was to return and pay for it. Then temptation came. First, it was only $4.95; they won't miss it. Second, we just spent a lot of money; they made enough on us. Third, the store is far from the car. Fourth, no one would know or care. After a brief struggle, I walked back and paid for the item. Why? Because I would have lost too much if I hadn't. I would have lost my self-respect and integrity. Otherwise, I'd be a shoplifter—a thief. Yes, no one would ever know, but God and I would. I would have never been able to look at the mirror and being proud of the person I saw again.

Knowing the importance of these four factors, we know they are easy to understand but hard to do. You need the Success Triangle to keep you on course.

The Success Triangle

As we embark on the journey to success, we'll meet roadblocks, detours, and setbacks. Sometimes we wonder how we can continue. Often it's easier to give up and say, "It's a stupid game," and quit. We need a system—the success triangle—to remind and keep us consistent and persistent on the path to success. See below:

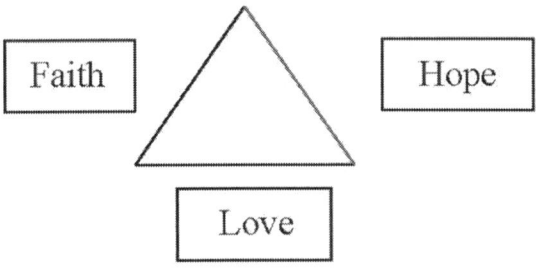

A triangle is the strongest structure known to man. The two sides are faith and hope. The base is love. If you seek money and fame, faith and hope will do. If you want true success, you need a strong base called love. At first glance, this may appear to be a mini sermon. The objective shows that while faith, hope, and love are important principles of the Christian faith, they are also important in the secular world. These basic tools help us win the invisible wars we fight every day.

Faith

Faith is the direct opposite of fear.

Once you have a vision and the desire to succeed, almost immediately you will be hit hard by the fear of failure. To succeed in any endeavor, you must begin with a leap of faith.

What is faith?

- Faith is a believing before seeing
- Faith is a belief system that creates your future in advance.
- Faith is daring to believe in your dreams, take a risk, and get going.

- Faith is daring to make a commitment and not look back when the going gets tough.

- Faith is a farmer daring to sow the last barrel of seeds, knowing that keeping them will feed him for a few days, but believing that sowing them may feed him for life.

- Faith is to continue believing in God, even when he is silent.

> Faith is the substance of things hope for,
> the evidence of things not seen
> —Hebrews 11:1

Great people are ordinary people with an extraordinary amount of faith.

"Seeing is believing!" A quote from Aristotle (350 BC).

This quote had led many people astray through the years! It made many people became skeptical on anything that is new and unusual! The truth is that we have to "believe it before we can see it". Besides this biblical truth, it is truth in science as well.

Faith and Science

Many think faith and science are not compatible. Nothing is farther from the truth. Every scientific discovery started with a hypothesis based on inductive or deductive reasoning. Before it's proven, the scientist must proceed on **faith**.

While I was at MIT in 1956, I took a course called Astronautical Guidance. The homework was to plot a course for a mission to Mars. I asked the professor what gravitational constant to use in deep space, as we had never been there before.

"Use the same constant we use on Earth, <u>by faith</u>." The professor shocked me. Then he added jokingly, "Be glad that you are an engineer, Bob, and not an astronaut whose life is dependent on your calculations."

Indeed, if we want to push the frontiers of science, we have to believe it before we see it.

Faith and our cosmos

With the aid of our new Hubble telescope, we can see farther into our universe. Now, let us analyze what we see:

"Seeing before believing!" Aristotle (350 BC)

1. This is the Earth! This is where you live.

NASAGoddard Space Flight Center Image / Via visibleearth.nasa.gov

2. But that's nothing compared to our sun.

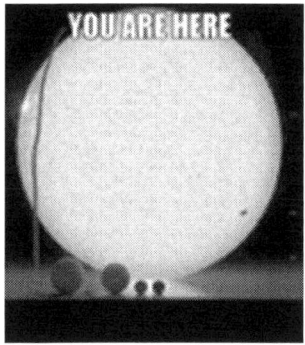

Via Twitter: @maiwandafghani

and everything you have ever known exists on that little speck.

3. Now, there are ones much, much bigger than little wimpy sun. The biggest star, VY Canis Majoris, is 1,000,000,000 times bigger than our sun:

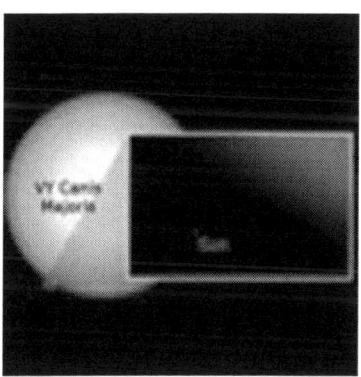

Via en.wikipedia.org

4. Now, let's look at the Milky Way galaxy. This is where our solar system is:

Via Twitter: @lucybrockle

5. But even our galaxy is a little runt compared with some others. Here's the Milky Way compared to IC 1011, 350 million light years away from Earth: Milky Way is just a little dot!

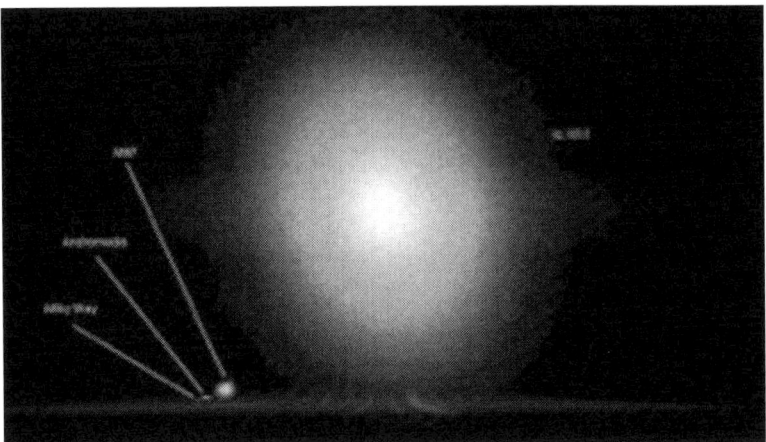

Via Twitter: @smokeinpublic

6. Now how about the "black holes" you can't even see? What lies inside them?

Passion

A famous British scientist saw the cosmos and exclaimed: "There is no God!" because he cannot find Him there!

Many other scientists see the immensity of the universe and the beauty around us and perceive that there must be a God! They also realize that we are just one out of 7,000,000.000. (7 Billion) people on this tiny earth; They got off their high horses and looked inside ourselves with faith they found God there!

"Believing before seeing..." Jesus Christ
"For we walk by faith, not by sight..." 2 Corinthian 5:7
Faith allows us to reach into the invisible world.

Christopher Columbus (1451-1506)

Christopher Columbus was an Italian explorer who sailed across the Atlantic Ocean in 1492 hoping to find a new route to India (to trade for spices). Columbus's desire to find a westward route to Asia grew out of his faith that the earth was round - a sphere, perhaps from the bible: Isaish 40:22, (that God is enthroned above the sphere of Earth) reinforced by his own observation. This is an unproven theory at the time.

Since he believed the earth was a sphere, he reasoned he should reach Asia by sailing in the opposite direction. He set his goals, made careful plans, and took his leap of faith. After considerable difficulties, he gained the support of the Spanish Catholic monarchs, Isabel and Fernando.

On his first trip, Columbus led an expedition with three ships, the Niña (captained by Vicente Yáñez Pinzon), the Pinta (owned and captained by Martin Alonzo Pinzon), and the Santa Maria (captained by Columbus), with about ninety crewmembers. They set sail on August 3, 1492, from Palos, Spain.

The widely published report of his voyage made Columbus famous throughout Europe, secured him the Admiral of the Ocean Sea title, and furthered royal patronage.

Columbus, who never abandoned the belief that he had reached India, led three more expeditions to the Caribbean. (Have you ever wondered why the American natives were called American Indians?)

After five centuries, Columbus remains a mysterious and controversial figure who has been variously described as one of the greatest mariners in history, a visionary genius, a mystic, a national hero, and a fellow who failed to reach his goal (India).

Regardless of what people say about him, one thing is sure. He had faith, set his goals, made his plans, and had the guts to risk his life to take action. Even though he never reached India, he found something far better: a new world! We have all benefited from his deeds.

Below is a true story from ancient China to illustrate the importance of using faith in one's judgments and having the guts to take action and overcome impossible odds.

The Strategy of the Empty City

Background: This is taken from the famous historical novel, The Story of Three Kingdoms, written five hundred years ago. The story took place around 200 AD, approximately 1,800 years ago. Kin-Ming was an outstanding military strategist and a scholar who later became the prime minister of his country, Han. Many battles were fought by the three kingdoms. Each time, the enemy was soundly defeated by Kon-Ming's superior strategies, so all the opposing army generals held him in awe. The story began when General Mar, one of Kon-Ming's generals who disobeyed his instructions, lost a great battle and exposed the entire right flank of Kon-Ming's army. Kon-Ming was able to survive against this impossible odds because he had faith in his own abilities and strategies but even more important was his faith in his understanding of his opponent's major weakness: **suspicion.**

Scene 1: In Kon-Ming's Camp inside the West City

A rider hastily galloped in and reported to Kon-Ming. "General Mar did not follow your instructions, sir. He did not build stockades (forts) to block the enemy's advance. Instead, he amassed his army on the mountains."

"Fools! This is mindless suicide," said Kon-Ming. "His act will endanger the whole army. He must be replaced at once! General Yang, replace him."

"Yes, sir! I'm on my way," answered the elderly General Yang. "I'll follow your plans and build the stockades."

Unfortunately, before General Yang left, three reports came in quick succession. "General Mar is surrounded, and the enemy has cut off his water supply," said the first runner.

"General Mar ordered the army to charge, but was repelled. He is waiting for reinforcements," said the second runner.

"General Mar's army has been completely destroyed. The enemy is pouring through in great strength. Our entire right flank is collapsing, and we're in danger of being surrounded by the enemy!" reported the third runner.

Realizing the gravity of the situation, Kon-Ming decided he should retreat to save the army. He quickly ordered two of his trusted generals to strengthen the right flank.

"Do your best to slow the enemy's advance. You must buy us some time to organize an orderly retreat," Kon-Ming said.

He then turned to his two young generals. "General Chang and General Kwan, each of you take three thousand soldiers and hide in the surrounding mountains to cover my retreat. Use many flags to disguise your strength. Do not engage the enemy unless absolutely necessary. Remember, they have great numerical superiority."

The two generals took their armies and left quickly.

Scene 2: Army Headquarters, West City, One Day Later

"Disaster! Mr. Prime Minister, the enemy with 150,000 strong is rapidly approaching the city," the out-of-breath runner cried.

"Oh, no! We've only 2,500 soldiers left in the city and not a single general," the officials cried. "We can't fight. We must run away quickly!"

"If we run, we are sure to be captured," said Kon-Ming. "We cannot outrun the cavalry."

He issued an order to the captain in charge. "I want you to make sure everyone in the hall keeps this news an absolute secret. Anyone who spreads fear will be cut down immediately. I want the whole city to be quiet as if nothing has happened," Kon-Ming told the captain.

"Here's my plan," Kon-Ming went on. "Its success depends on the faith of the training and discipline of our troops and on my understanding of the strength and weakness of the enemy's commander."

Kon-Ming sent twenty-four soldiers dressed as civilians with instructions to sweep the ground outside the city gate as if they didn't have a care in the world. He ordered the city gate be left wide open. He told his musicians to play loud, happy music on the city walls above the gate.

"Now, everyone, relax. I'm ready for the enemy," Kon-Ming said as he sat among the pale faces of his frightened staff.

Scene 3: At the City Gate

As Kon-Ming sat above the city gate with his musicians playing happy music, the vanguard of the enemy arrived.

"Halt!" the vanguard captain ordered. "They are neither fighting nor retreating. They left the gate open and have totally ignored us. Quick! Report this strange situation to the commanding general."

When the commanding general came to see the situation, Kon-Ming appeared on the wall above the gate. "General, we're expecting you. We've prepared a good meal and fine wine. We are waiting for you to join me at a concert," Kon-Ming said, smiling. "Please come in and join us."

Having been caught in many of Kon-Ming's tricks and traps, the commanding general smelled another ambush and quickly ordered his army to retreat.

As the enemy was retreating, Kon-Ming's two young generals who were hiding in the hills and saw Kon-Ming's desperate situation. They ordered their small army to conduct a kamikaze-like attack into the retreating hordes. Their attack confirmed the enemy's fear that they had fallen into a trap, so they scattered and ran. The two young generals won a great victory and captured many weapons, warhorses, and supplies while Kon-Ming retreated orderly to safety.

Scene 4: Kon-Ming's Camp in his Homeland

"Oh, what a victory!" General Chang said, "With 6,000 against 150,000, we routed them!"

"They abandoned their supplies and ran like chickens!" said General Kwan. "Ha! Ha! They were in a total panic. I've never had a sweeter victory."

"You were a genius, Prime Minister," the officials said. "Turning a disaster into an incredible victory is nothing short of a miracle."

"I still cannot understand why the enemy retreated with such a strong army," General Chang said.

"When a bird has been shot at many times, the mere sound of the bow will send it fleeing," said Kon-Ming. "The enemy general knew I was a very cautious man and do not like to take chances. What he did not know was that I had no army to fight with, and neither could I run away. I was desperate, and my only choice was to put up a front. Fortunately, it worked."

Epilogue: When the enemy general was informed later about the true situation, he said, "Kon-Ming is truly a genius. I'm no match for him. Fortunately, he has some incompetent generals."

Food for Thought: When you think you have exhausted all possibilities, you haven't.

God gives us an all-powerful mind. Use it. Never give up!

Note: To be historically accurate, Kon-Ming's real name was Zhūgé Liàng (諸葛亮), nickname Kon-Ming (孔明). Zhūgé was his last name. Kon-Ming or Kongming was the name used in the English translation of the book, Three Kingdoms (University of California Press). Kon-Ming was also commonly known and used in most Chinese stories.

Hope

Once we have taken the leap of faith, we'll encounter obstacles and may often fail. Yes, fail. We need hope to sustain us. Hope helps us to be consistent and persistent.

> **F*ailure is the mother of success*.**
> —A *Chinese proverb*

Many people have the mistaken notion that if we work hard, we'll eventually succeed. Unfortunately, this is no longer true in today's economy. If we work hard all our lives at a job, we may not even get a gold watch when and if we reach retirement age.

The true secret of success is always being open to opportunities and never quit trying. If one thing did not work, try something new. In other words, try to work smarter and find new ways to solve your problem. Never give up!

Famous Failures (Read "Built to Last" Ref.7 Appendix D for the full stories.)

- The 3M Company began with a corundum mine that failed. They hung on and eventually succeeded with wet-dry sandpaper. Do you know that the famous 3M Post-it notes came from a failed superglue experiment?

- The famous Hewlett-Packard Company (HP) started with a failed bowling foul-line indicator and a failed automatic urinal flusher. They had good ideas, but were way ahead of their time. The vacuum tube technology, just couldn't cut it. By hanging on with hope, they got their break when the Disney Company awarded them a contract for eight oscilloscopes for the film Fantasia.

- The Sony Company started with a rice cooker that failed to work properly. Their sweetened bean paste soup, heating pads, and first tape recorder also failed in the marketplace.

- The Boeing Company's first seaplane failed to pass the navy's test; they had to go into the furniture business to stay alive.

All the leaders of these world-famous companies succeeded by staying true to their company's core belief, never quitting, and always hanging on to hope. For example, HP's core belief is "Technological innovation and making a contribution to society." It has nothing to do with the automatic urinal flusher. If one product does not work, try something else.

Success is never ending. Failure is never final.
—Dr. Robert H. Schuller

Hope is staying the course against all odds, hoping that things will work out as planned though the going gets tough. The farmer keeps working the farm in bad weather, hoping the seeds he planted will multiply. The cancer patient keeps hoping tomorrow will come.

> Defeat may be victory in disguise;
> the lowest ebb is the turn of the tide.
> —Henry Wadsworth Longfellow

***There's no hopeless situation,* if you do not give up!**

Hope is one of the most important ingredients for success. No matter what you started, sooner or later, you'll face impossible problems. To solve them, you must recognize that in fighting an invisible war, the battleground is in your mind. You have two choices: hope or worry.

Hope Is the Direct Opposite of Worry

Hope focuses on and magnifies your goal, faith, and vision and minimizes your problems.

Worry magnifies your problems. It is a negative force that will generate fear and paralyze you into inaction, despair, and depression. Eventually, it can lead to self-destruction. Many suicides and murder/suicides occur when people give up and seek a quick end to their problems.

On the other hand, hope is a positive force that will drive us into continuous action to face our problems head-on and solve them. Hope allows us to hang on, knowing that with time, "this too will pass."

One of the best ways of holding onto hope is to remember the following:

The Possibility Thinker's Creed

When faced with a mountain,
I will not quit!
I will keep on striving until I climb over,
find a pass through, or simply stay and
turn my mountain into a gold mine,
with God's help.
—Dr. Robert H. Schuller

Columbus Story (continued)

As we mentioned, Columbus's faith got him going. Hope sustained him.

Since Columbus's first voyage was exploration and discovery, and no one knew what was ahead, the ships carried enough provisions for one year.

Compasses, astrolabes, hourglasses, maps, and charts were the most important navigational aids at that time. Celestial navigation was the favored method while sailing under familiar stars, but dead reckoning was more dependable in East–West voyages in unknown seas.

In dead reckoning, a pilot calculated the speed of the ship by measuring the time it took a floating device to travel the ship's known length from the bow to the stern. The compass, whose magnetized needle was supposed to point in the direction of the North Star, worked well in the Mediterranean, Indian Ocean, and Eastern waters.

After several weeks in the Atlantic, however, the crew became alarmed when the compass needles on all three ships deviated from true north to a few degrees west. Columbus quelled their fears by explaining the variation was due to the instability of the North Star. Like other stars, he explained (perhaps with his fingers crossed), this one moved. Fortunately, the crew bought the explanation.

After thirty-four days on the open sea without signs of life, the sailors became hysterical and were ready for mutiny. They believed that the earth was flat and that at any moment they would fall off.

Columbus held on to his belief the earth was round and convinced the potential mutineers to wait three more days because he knew (hoped) land was near. Fortunately, the next day they spotted tree branches, and the rest is history.

When you think you have reached the end of your rope, *don't give up; tie a knot and hang on!*

A Personal Lesson on Hope

Attending a possibility thinking church often challenges a person to try different ideas and develop projects. In the seventies, I ventured and formed a group. We purchased three and a half acres of rural land in Lake Forest, California, and built a modern, forty-lane bowling center called Forest Lanes.

It was exciting to watch this forty-thousand-square-foot building emerge from ground breaking to finish. I knew little about the management problems associated with a complex operation that had more than forty employees.

As the company's president and CEO, I was awakened at two o'clock in the morning with a panicked call from the assistant manager. The general manager and head mechanic were coming to blows during an argument. They were both outstanding bowlers and preferred different lane conditions. Both insisted they were right.

I interviewed them separately and found they both loved their jobs and the facility. I told them to go home and sleep it off, and I would meet them at noon the next day. As they were both indispensable to the business, I had a real problem.

The next morning as I was having my morning devotion, I came across this passage. "He shall be like a tree planted by the rivers of water, that brings forth fruit in its season, *whose leaves also shall not wither. And whatsoever he does shall prosper*" (Psalm 1:3).

I prayed earnestly that God would make me be like that tree. The answer came swiftly in my mind: "Bob, You are like that tree. You think the tree is in a blessed position because you can see the infinite supply of nutrients from the river. But pity the poor tree; it sees only what its roots can feel. In the winter, it thinks that it will starve, and in the spring, it thinks that it will drown. All the time it's in the most blessed position."

From then on, every time I faced big problems, I thought about that tree in winter, hoping and waiting for summer to come soon.

Every problem has a solution if you have hope and hang on!

Incidentally, we identified that the big blowup came from the accumulation of small conflicts between the two departments. Compromises and a system of communications were worked out, and we had a big laugh later. (An important age-old Chinese management principle: break a big problem into smaller problems and manage the small problems away.)

Faith plus hope will make you a financial or material success, but if your base—love– is weak, the triangle can easily topple. That's why many people achieve fame and fortune while their own lives are a mess. Read the daily newspapers, the supermarket tabloids and watch the evening news; you'll know what I mean.

Love

Love is the desire to provide valuable services to mankind. The action of love moves you from success into significance.

If you want to make a good living, faith and hope will do. If you want to build a good life, you need love—not love in words but in deeds.

There are many kinds of love: sacrificial love, romantic love, and self-love. We'll concentrate on sacrificial love, which is also called agape love.

Love Is the Opposite of Greed (Envy)

People will remember Bill Gates not because of his multi-billion net worth; but because of his $32 billion foundation for health and education. Recently, his foundation offered a thousand fellowships to deserving minority college students. This is akin to planting a thousand fruit trees on the earth; the world will eat from his action for centuries to come.

Paul Getty was not remembered for his oil fortune, but he will be remembered for the Getty Art Museum, a gift to the world to preserve fine arts for the future generations.

Walt Disney wrote his story with love in the hearts of children of all ages everywhere.

These people are real successes because they gave out of love in deeds for their fellow people.

Love is not love until it is given away.

Below are more stories on this matter

George Washington at Valley Forge

Following your dream is never easy. Think of the Continental Congress on July 4, 1776. What did they have? Nothing was in place: no money, formal organization, or established government. They had only a vision and a belief in a bright tomorrow.

George Washington was a rich gentleman farmer. His whole motivation for serving his country was not for money or fame. He did it because he loved his country, had a vision, and wanted to contribute.

A Story Called the "Five Noes"

Legend has it that when George Washington was given the command of the Continental Army, one of his friends, a British sympathizer, came to him at night and asked him five questions.

1. Do you have a trained army? The answer was no.

2. Do you have all the guns and cannons you need? The answer was no.

3. Do you have enough money to pay your soldiers? The answer was no.

4. Is everybody behind you? The answer was no.

5. With all those "noes," are you out of your mind? The answer was no!

In 1777, Washington led his troops to Valley Forge, Pennsylvania, after recent defeats at Philadelphia and Germantown. His soldiers had little food, supplies, or clothing for the winter. The army of eleven thousand lived in crude huts they built themselves.

On December 23, 1777, Washington wrote, "We've this day, no less than 2,873 men not fit for duty because they are barefooted and otherwise naked."

More than three thousand soldiers died during that period. Many others were too weak or too sick to fight because of a smallpox epidemic. Others went home. The winter at Valley Forge tested the faith, hope, and love of the American troops. Only the dedicated patriots stayed. Despite the incredible odds, these people helped build a nation!

Recorded history shows us that good old George didn't defeat the British by winning many battles. By never quitting, he drove the British crazy. He had too much love for his country to ever quit.

Benedict Arnold at West Point

Benedict Arnold was one of Washington's best generals. He was a brave and good commander. Washington treated him like a son. As a result, he gave Benedict Arnold an important assignment: building a fort at West Point to stop the British from coming up the Hudson River.

After Washington's multiple defeats, Benedict Arnold lost his faith and hope. Since he wasn't ready to give his life for the love of his country, he quit and gave the plans to a British spy. Unfortunately (or fortunately), the spy was caught before he could deliver them. The rest is history.

Same opportunity, two completely different outcomes!

> Kindness in words creates confidence.
> Kindness in thinking creates profoundness.
> Kindness in giving creates love.
> —Lao-Tze (sixth century BC)

Mother Teresa's Missionaries of Charity (Love)

During her lifetime and after her death, Mother Teresa was consistently found by the Gallup Poll to be the single most widely admired person. In 1999, she was ranked as the "most admired person of the 20th century." Volumes have been written about this slightly built, remarkable woman.

A brief history of Mother Teresa

In October 1950, Mother Teresa received the Vatican's permission to start a diocesan congregation, which became the Missionaries of Charity, whose vocation was to care for (in her words) "the hungry, the naked, the homeless, the crippled, the blind, the lepers, all those people who feel unwanted, unloved, and uncared for throughout society."

The Missionaries of Charity began with thirteen members in Calcutta. Today the order has more than four thousand nuns running orphanages, AIDS hospices, and charity centers worldwide. It cares for refugees, the blind, disabled, aged, alcoholics, the poor and homeless, and victims of floods, epidemics, and famine on all six continents.

Mother Teresa opened the first Home for the Dying in the city of Calcutta in 1952. By the 1960s, she had opened hospices, orphanages, and leper houses throughout India. She was one of the first to establish homes for AIDS victims. New homes opened around the globe: Venezuela, Rome, Tanzania, and eventually in Asia, Africa, and Europe. By 1996, she operated 517 missions in more than a hundred countries.

In 1971, Pope Paul VI awarded her the first Pope John XXIII Peace Prize. Other awards bestowed on her included a Kennedy Prize (1971); the Nehru Prize for promotion of international peace and understanding (1972); the Balzan Prize (1979) for humanity, peace, and brotherhood among people; the Albert Schweitzer International Prize (1975); the United States Presidential Medal of Freedom (1985) and Congressional Gold Medal (1994); honorary citizenship of the United States (November 16, 1996); and honorary degrees from a number of universities.

In 1979, Mother Teresa was awarded the Nobel Peace Prize "for work undertaken in the struggle to overcome poverty and distress, which also constitute a threat to peace." She refused the conventional ceremonial banquet given to laureates, and asked that the six thousand dollars be diverted to the Calcutta poor, claiming the money would permit her to feed hundreds of needy for a year. When Mother Teresa received the prize, she was asked what we can do to promote world peace. Her answer was simple: *"Go home and love your family."*

In 1982, Mother Teresa persuaded Israelis and Palestinians, in the midst of a skirmish, to cease fire long enough to rescue thirty-seven mentally handicapped patients from a besieged Beirut hospital.

When the walls of Eastern Europe collapsed, she expanded her efforts to Communist countries.

She was undeterred by criticism about her firm stand against abortion and divorce, saying, "No matter who says what, you should accept it with a smile and do your own work." (See her poem, Do It Anyway, in Chapter 2.)

Her sisters say the peace prayer of St. Francis every morning before breakfast. Many of the vows and emphasis of her ministry are similar. St. Francis emphasized poverty, chastity, obedience, and submission to Christ. St. Francis devoted much of his life to the service of the poor, especially lepers in the area where he lived.

(Reference source: http://en.wikipedia.org/wiki/Mother_Teresa#Spiritual_life.)

Prayer of St. Francis of Assisi

Lord, make me an instrument of your peace;
Where there is hatred, let me sow love;
Where there is injury, pardon;
Where there is doubt, faith;

Where there is despair, hope;
Where there is darkness, light;
Where there is sadness, joy.

O Divine Master, grant that I may not so much seek
to be consoled as to console,
To be understood as to understand,
To be loved as to love.

For it is in giving that we receive.
It is in pardoning that we are pardoned,
And it is in dying that we are born to eternal life.

Many people will say, "We are not like these great people. How can our love make a difference?"

For us ordinary people, the best example of sacrificial love is exhibited by a mother and her baby. A mother is the only one who can sing while changing a diaper. Many mothers will willingly give their own lives to save their babies. Mothers also know their babies are not perfect. Each has an end she kisses and an end she wipes. If one mixes the two ends, the baby isn't very interesting.

This is true in human relationships. If we understand that nobody is perfect and note that there's the good part you kiss and the bad part you have to accept. Once we understand this principle, fewer divorces and broken relationships would happen.

Love Is her Diploma

Background: This true story happened in Hong Kong—still under British rule— during the Cultural Revolution in China (1966 to 1976.) During the Cultural Revolution, most Chinese schools were closed for up to ten years. Refugees poured in from China.

Many were well-educated school principals, professors, and teachers fearing persecution. Because jobs were scarce, many children were abandoned by their families. The British government had a big headache taking care of the situation.

* * *

Susie combed her hair. She was apprehensive. This was her first job interview. In her twenty-nine years, she had been mostly raised in an orphanage. When she was eighteen, she chose to work in the orphanage instead of looking for a job. She loved her work and loved the children.

Occasionally she had nightmares about an experience when she was abandoned at age four. She remembered well that morning as they ran from a bombing raid. Her father carried her two-year-old brother and told her to hang on to his shirt as they ran. Many people hurried and pushed, and she was separated from her father.

"Daddy!" she screamed as she was pushed aside. She was helpless, hungry, and cold. She was so frightened at night that she cried herself to sleep. She was comforted by her mother's story that a big angel always comes to save little children. Every morning as the day's light peeked through the trees, she strained her eyes, hoping to see her father and brother come for her. She soon gave up hope.

One day, Mama Wong, head of the orphanage, appeared like an angel and literally picked her up and gave her life and hope. Susie secretly promised she would never leave Mama

Wong, and she would be an angel and help her and the lost children.

Mama Wong told her to interview for the job as head of a new orphanage. Susie felt unqualified for the job. Many refugees in Hong Kong were ex-school principals, professors, and child specialists and would interview for this one job.

I *don't even have a* high school diploma. All I have is a letter of recommendation from Mama Wong. What good is that? Susie thought. "Oh! I wish this hair would stay down," she muttered.

Fortunately, the bus arrived.

As she rushed to go upstairs for the interview, she spied a little girl, two or three years old, crying at the bottom of the staircase.

"Where's your mama?" Susie asked.

The little girl said nothing.

Susie looked around. She saw an old man outside read a newspaper by the bus stop. "Do you know where this little girl's mother is?"

The old man shrugged and continued reading his newspaper.

Susie returned to the girl and wiped her tears with her handkerchief. She gave her a hug and a small piece of candy.

"Don't worry," Susie said. "Jiě jiě" (Chinese for big sister) will help you find your mama. Sit here. I'll be back to take care of you."

The interview was uneventful. After a few routine questions, it was finished. She handed in her recommendation letter and hurried downstairs.

"Are you lost?" Susie said as she picked up the girl. The girl gave no reply. Apparently, she couldn't talk; she only nodded or shook her head.

After using all her tricks to calm the girl, Susie discovered a telephone number on the inside hem of the little girl's dress. With a big sigh of relief, Susie picked up the girl and went back upstairs to ask the secretary about using her phone. When she dialed the number, the phone in the next room rang.

As the door opened, the interview group showed up and congratulated her on getting the job.

"What?" the startled Susie exclaimed. "I'm the least qualified for the job."

As it turned out, the little girl was a plant. They chose the dirtiest, most troublesome girl from the orphanage and put her downstairs under the watchful eye of the old man, who pretended to be reading the newspaper. None of the applicants responded to the girl or chose not to see her.

"When you returned again to help her, we knew we had the right person," said the boss.

"Still, I'm not qualified. I don't even have a diploma," Susie said again.

"In this job, we are not looking for a piece of paper. We are looking at the heart. Look at your recommendation letter."

It said: "To Whom It May Concern: Susie came to me when she was four years old. She was abandoned because of the war. I already had too many children to care for. I could not take on another child. Her irresistible smile and sparkling bright eyes totally disarmed me. Even at that age, she had a calming effect on the other small children.

"She attended the orphanage school, taught by the nuns. She is smart and learns quickly. She can read and write well. In the past twenty-five years, Susie has learned every aspect of running an orphanage. When I had an operation a few years ago, I put Susie in charge. She did an excellent job. She cares and cares. Even though she has no formal education, truly, *love is her diploma."*

In love's service, only b**roken hearts will do!**

Did I fill the world with love?

A song from "Good-bye, Mr. Chips"

In the morning of my life I shall look to the sunrise.
At a moment in my life when the world is new, And the
blessing I shall ask is that God will grant me,
To be brave and strong and true,
And to fill the world with love my whole life through.

In the noontime of my life I shall look to the sunshine.
At a moment in my life when the sky is blue,
And the blessing I shall ask shall remain unchanging.
To be brave and strong and true,
And to fill the world with love my whole life through.

In the evening of my life I shall look to the sunset.
At a moment in my life when the night is due,

And the question I shall ask only I can answer.
Was I brave and strong and true?
Did I fill the world with love my whole life through?

The lyric is included in loving remembrance of my good friend, Fred Frank, a famous soloist of the Hour of Power and the Crystal Cathedral. It was one of his favorite songs.

The Tender Trap

Here's a story to illustrate what <u>love is not</u>. It's included because this is happening to someone somewhere every day.

These days divorce is common, and commitment is rare. Almost every day, one can read about problems with young people abusing drugs, sex, alcohol, and getting into trouble with the law. Misguided love builds a tender trap.

"Pastor! You've got to help me. I'm at the end of my rope!" the woman cried as she entered the pastor's office, sobbing.

"Please sit down," the pastor said, pointing to a nearby chair. "Are you a member of the congregation?" He did not recognize her.

"No. You've got to help me! He's been arrested for armed robbery. He's in jail. You've got to help me!" the woman wailed.

"Calm down. What's your name and who was being arrested?" the pastor asked.

"My name is Cathy," the woman said as she dried her tears with her hand and tried to straighten her messy hair. "My son, Joe, was arrested in college for armed robbery a couple of days ago. As he was on probation, they denied him bail. I couldn't afford bail. He called to tell me the prisoners are abusing him. What should I do?"

"Take it easy. Drink this coffee, and tell me all about it," the pastor said. "Start from the beginning."

"Joe's father left us when Joe was a few months old. He left me with a house and a big mortgage payment. I had to work to make ends meet. I reluctantly left Joe with the nursery during the day, which made me feel guilty when I picked him up every evening. I spent every waking moment with him to care of his every need. I rocked him to sleep every night because he wanted it, and I needed it because I was lonely. When he was two, Joe started sucking his fingers. People told me that it was because he felt insecure. Those comments made me felt even guiltier. I promised him Mama would care for his every need. He'll never have to feel unwanted or insecure."

"When he was old enough and tried to tie his shoes but ended up with a dead knot, what did you do?" the pastor asked.

"I tried to teach him a few times with no success," the mother answered. "Joe cries when he's frustrated, so I bought him Velcro shoes. It was not that important to learn to tie his shoes."

"How old was he when he learned to read the clock?" "I tried to teach him a few times, so I thought why bother with the obsolete idea and bought him a digital clock and watch. They are much cheaper."

"When did he learn multiplication?"

"That's hard and outdated. I bought him a calculator instead.

"When did he learn to read?"

"His teacher was incompetent and insensitive to his needs. She sent a note telling me that he was not attentive in class and should be disciplined. I told her he was a good boy, but cried when he was frustrated. She mustn't be so hard on him. She never paid any special attention to him again. That's why he never learned to read very well."

"Does he play sports?"

"Oh, no. I don't want to ruin his fingers. He plays the piano, you know."

"He is a classical pianist?"

"No, but Joe is talented. He can pick out a tune by himself and attacks the piano with emotion and gusto. I tried to have him take piano lessons, but he came back crying that the teacher only wanted to teach him hand positions and gave him difficult, old music. 'I already know how to play, and I hate dead men's music,' Joe complained. I didn't like the dead men's music either. I figured that as long as he was happy, having fun, and was popular with his friends, it was okay with me."

"Does he have any girlfriends?"

"Lots! The girls literally throw themselves at him. I tried to tell him about sex and diseases, but he told me they already taught him in school about safe sex and how to be careful."

"How did you pick this particular college?"

"Joe was never a good student. His SAT score was low, and he couldn't get into college. I never got a college education, but I thought Joe must get a good education so that he'll have a good start in life. This was the only college that accepted him, provided he took the additional tutoring in math and English. It was expensive, so I took out a second mortgage to send him there."

"What happened then?"

"After Joe went to college, in all his letters he asked for money. He needed money for new books, new clothes, etc. I gave him every dime I had and even sold my wedding ring. When I told him there was no more money, the letters stopped. I called him at the dorm, but there was no answer, even at midnight.

"I was concerned, so I visited him. This college turned out to be one big partying machine. Most students are from well-to-do families, and they were there because they do not want to study. There were parties every night in different fraternities and sororities. Joe was always the life of the party.

"He learned to drink, smoke, and take drugs. He slept with different girls every night. That's why he was never in his room. I warned him that if he didn't straighten out, I'd cut off his support."

"Then what happened?"

"The next thing I knew, he was caught shoplifting. I took out a third mortgage to bail him out. One month later, he was caught doing armed robbery. He told me he needed the money for the drugs, or the dealers would kill him. Because one victim was hurt in the robbery and he was on probation, they denied him bail. Joe cries to me that the other prisoners are abusing him. What do I do?"

The pastor took a long sip of his coffee, let out a deep sigh, and said to Cathy, "I'm sorry that I have no solutions for you. Joe is a victim of what I call the "tender trap." In our modern, permissive society, many people are in your same shoes. You see, there are so many single parents these days. Many are depressed that they often drown their sorrows in alcohol and/or drugs. Many others like you felt so guilty for having to leave their children to go to work that they become overly permissive. Their children are literally raised like pets. They forget that the job of parenting is to discipline, teach, and inspire."

<u>Misguided love builds a tender trap.</u>

"But there must be a way to save Joe," said Cathy. "I'll do anything."

"You can make a young tree grow straight by tying it to a stick. When it grows older and crooked, not much can be done," replied the pastor.

"Does it mean that there is no hope?" Cathy replied.

"There is always hope if you have faith. I suggest that we try prayer."

Comment: What we do in life echoes in eternity. It's not just Joe's life that was ruined; imagine what Joe's children and grandchildren will be like.

The Bible says "Chasten your son while there is hope, and do not set your heart on his destruction" (Proverbs 19:18).

In this modern world, many people consider the teachings of the Bible old-fashioned and no longer applicable. Many parents want to transfer the responsibility of raising their children to schoolteachers. When the children fail, they blame the teacher. In the meantime, they want more teachers and blame the shortage on the lack of government funding. Raising children is an impossible task for the teachers because they have neither the time nor the ability to supervise them outside the classroom.

Many single parents have a difficult time caring for the children, but many succeed when they understand that to love their kids includes discipline, education, challenge, and inspiration.

We build our children;
our children build our future.
It is important we build our children
one day at a time!

A True Story of the Success Triangle

– The Nick Vujicic Story: From Life without Limbs to Life without Limits

When I first heard of Nick Vujicic, a man born without limbs who was barely three feet tall, coming to be interviewed at our church service at the Crystal Cathedral, my first impression was, "Wow! This must be an extremely unusual story."

As I walked into our church on the day of his interview, Nick Vujicic sat in his electric wheelchair, talking to people at the back of the church. He seemed to be an extremely outgoing, intelligent, and friendly person.

Passion

A picture of Nick Vujicic and the author on the grounds of the Crystal Cathedral

When the service was about to start, he navigated his electric wheelchair confidently down the long, narrow aisle to the front and greeted the people.

During his interview, he had to be placed on top of a table. He spoke eloquently and presented himself well. He told his powerful story and gave his testimony about how he found his purpose in life. At the end, he was given a standing ovation. In fact, most of us were so impressed that we wished he could have stayed and preached a sermon.

Nick Vujicic was born on the morning of the fourth of December 1982, in Melbourne, Australia. His parents, both lifelong Christians, had eagerly anticipated the birth of their first child.

Alas, he came without limbs. There were no warnings to prepare them for the situation. The doctors were shocked and had no answers. There is still no medical reason why this happened. His parents were absolutely devastated, in shock, and confused.

Understandably, Nick's parents had strong concern and fears about what kind of life he could lead. It took them a number of months of tears, questions, and grief before complete faith and trust overtook their hearts. God taught them the meaning of true love and sacrifice and provided them with hope, strength, wisdom, and courage through those early years.

At the time of Nick's starting school, the Australian education system was revising the law of segregation of special needs children. Nick Vujicic was used as the example of a disabled child being integrated successfully into a mainstream school.

In his early school years, he encountered uncomfortable times of feeling rejected and bullied because of his physical difference. With his parents' support and love, he develops attitudes and values that helped him overcome the challenging times. He knew he was different, but on the inside, he was like everyone else.

Due to his emotional struggles, he experienced self-esteem problems and loneliness. God has implanted a passion of sharing his story and experiences to help others cope with whatever challenge they had in their lives, and he let God turn him into a blessing.

Nick Vujicic gave his life completely to Christ at the age of fifteen after reading the Gospel of John, Chapter 9. Jesus said that the reason the man was born blind was "so that the works of God may be revealed through him." Nick believed God would heal him so that he could be a great testimony of God's awesome power. Later on, Nick was given the wisdom to understand that if we pray for something, if it's God's will, it will happen in his time. If it's not God's will for it to happen, then he has something better.

Nick has complete peace knowing God won't let anything happen to him unless he has a good purpose for it. Nick believes his job is to encourage and to inspire others to live to their fullest potentials and not let anything hinder them in accomplishing their hopes and dreams.

Despite his handicaps, Nick Vujicic has completed a bachelor of commerce degree, majoring in financial planning and accounting. He has one small deformed foot that he calls "my chicken drumstick." He uses that to work the computer and can type forty-three words per minute. Nick is also a motivational speaker and loves to share his story and testimony at available opportunities. Nick has developed talks that relate to and encourage students through challenging topics for today's teenagers. He's now also a speaker in the corporate sector.

Recently, Nick was invited to speak in China about his faith, hope, and love. He spoke at churches and schools, including the Tsinghua University (the MIT of China) to thousands of students there and was very well received. (See www.youtube.com/watch?v=s5WlD0PMYt0)

In recent years, Nick has learned to become independent and can take care of all his personal needs. He can brush his teeth, comb his hair, dress, take care of his personal hygiene, and even shave. He gets around the house by jumping. Outside the house, Nick travels in a customized electric wheelchair. Nick loves to swim, fish, and play soccer. How do you fish if you don't have arms? He has a fishing rod with an electronic reel. Playing soccer? Where there's a will, there's a way! Nick Vujicic believes that "I can do all things through Christ who strengthens me" (Philippians 4:13).

Nick has a passion for reaching out to youth and to keep himself available for whatever God wants him to do. Here are some excerpts of Nick's sayings. "Take courage, my friend, for the battle is the Lord's, and I urge you to keep striving for the truth. For it is the truth that will set you free, and the peace of God, that surpasses all understanding, will reign in your hearts. May the Lord bless you as you diligently seek Him and grant you with godly wisdom and strength through your life's journey.

"The greatest impatience we experience in our walks with Christ are unanswered prayers. It feels that God doesn't care anymore. We all go through life's storms, and sometimes we feel helpless and hopeless. It's hard to understand, with our limited wisdom, why our loving God would let bad things happen in our lives. I thought, 'If He loves me that much, why does he let me feel so much pain?' I question God's existence, let alone His love for me. We doubt the credibility of Jeremiah 29:11, 'For I know the plans I have for you, declares the Lord, plans to prosper you and not to harm you, plans to give you hope and a future.'

"Sometimes our pain, suffering, anxiety, and depression seem more real than the promises of God. I share how God turned my life around from a life without limbs to a life without limits.

"God is using me in a mighty way to challenge people to claim the promise of that future and hope. As Proverbs 3:5 says, 'Trust the Lord with all your heart without understanding the circumstances in your life. God is a good God, not because of your circumstances, but because God is faithful and will not leave you.'

"It gives me no greater satisfaction than knowing that my life has a great purpose and can be used to glorify God. My prayer is that you'd be encouraged and challenged to seek diligently the Lord with all your heart and see the great future and hope you have in Christ. May God continue to strengthen and nurture your heart, according to His perfect will! Have a wonderful day knowing that God is with you every step of the way."

Paul Colman, a Christian music artist, said, "If the size of a man's capacity lies in his heart and spirit, then Nick Vujicic is a giant of a man. He's tenacious, captivating, and enthralling. I could not endorse another human being more highly."

> And now abide faith, hope, love, these three:
> but the greatest of these is LOVE.
> —1 Corinthian 13:13

A recent miracle is that Nick got married in 2011, and they have a baby! For more details, please go to: ww.lifewithoutlimbs.org.

Passion

Vision Accompanied with the "Success Triangle" creates PASSION!

The following three stories are people who have a passion for what they do.

The Bill Gates Story (Continued from chapter 1)

When Bill Gates's first company, Traf-O-Data, failed, he could have quit and returned to Harvard. He did not because his vision of the coming of the microchips was so strong that he truly believed it would revolutionize the computer industry and replace giant computers.

In 1974, Intel came up with the 8080 chip, which had 2,700 more transistors than the 8008 and ten times the capability. It cost only two hundred dollars.

Bill Gates and his partner, Paul Allen, saw the potential. They got busy writing software for the new Intel chip. In 1975, they formed a company to write and market their software for the microchip. Eventually they called the company Microsoft, meaning software for the microchip. They had a vision that this microchip would make computers, personal and affordable to everyone. The big computer firms, such as IBM, GE, RCA, Xerox, etc., with their staff of Ph.Ds didn't consider the microchip as a threat.

The Bible says, "Without vision, the people perish!" GE, RCA, and Xerox are no longer in the computer business. Do you know that Xerox invented the mouse and the graphic interface? The management at Xerox didn't know what they had and gave this "toy" to Apple Computer to play with. Bill Gates recognized the potential of this innovation right away, started working with Apple Computers, and later developed his own version called Microsoft Windows that took the world by storm.

Twenty years later, by 1995, Microsoft had seventeen thousand employees and was a business worth $6 billion per year. Bill Gates became the richest man in the world.

I admire Bill Gates not for the fortune he has accumulated but for his new vision to build a better world. His $35-billion foundation, working together with the billions contributed by Warren Buffett, will make a huge difference in world health and education for decades to come.

The Walt Disney Story

Walt was known as a dreamer who dared to reach for his impossible dreams. He was known as a pioneer, an innovator, and the possessor of one of the most fertile imaginations the world has known. He received more than 950 honors and awards from almost every nation. He received forty-eight Academy Awards and seven Emmys in his lifetime.

In 1918, Walt tried to enlist for military service in World War I. He was rejected because he was underage at sixteen. When one door closed, Walt opened another. He joined the Red Cross as an ambulance driver in France. His ambulance was covered with his cartoons.

Upon his return from France, he went into commercial art. Because of his lack of marketing skills, his company, Laugh-O-Gram, went bankrupt. He had to eat baked beans out of the cans. Instead of being discouraged by his failure, it inoculated him against the fear of failure. He traveled to Hollywood later, and with the help of his brother, Roy, and $250, he set up shop in his uncle's garage. Soon Mickey Mouse was born.

In 1937, Walt had a new vision. He wanted to produce the first full-length, animated feature film called Snow White and the Seven Dwarfs. The cost would be $1.5 million to produce. In the depth of the Great Depression, most people thought he would never raise the money and had gone off the deep end. As it turned out, the film was a great success. It is still considered one of the great feats and imperishable movie monuments that put the Walt Disney Studios among the elite of the movie industry.

In 1945, Walt pioneered another innovative idea: combining live action with cartoons. The Three Caballeros, Song of the South, and Mary Poppins were typical successes.

In 1955, Walt dared to reach for another impossible dream. He opened a Magic Kingdom at a cost of $17 million in a little town called Anaheim in California. Again, his critics left quietly as he entertained millions in his theme park, including kings and queens and royalty from over the world.

In 1965, Walt became concerned with improving the quality of urban lives in America. He wanted to develop an Experimental Prototype Community of Tomorrow (EPCOT Center). He purchased forty-three square miles of swampland (twice the size of Manhattan Island) in the middle of Florida. Many critics laughed at him again, saying mosquitoes and alligators don't buy tickets. Walt had the last laugh. Walt Disney World opened on schedule on October 1, 1971, and EPCOT Center opened on October 1, 1982.

Prior to his death on December 5, 1966, Walt wanted to help establish the California Institute of the Arts. "The principal thing I want to leave when I move on to greener pastures is to provide a place to develop the talents of the future, I think then I will have accomplished something," Walt once said.

Even on his deathbed, Walt was putting finishing touches on his last projects.

What drove him? Certainly not wealth or fame; he had plenty of that. I firmly believe he was driven by his passion for his work and his love for his fellow men.

By his contribution, he wrote his story in the hearts of children of all ages in almost every corner of the planet.

The Steve Jobs Story

It was sad to hear about the untimely passing of Steve Jobs at age of only 56. The world mourned and shared its admiration and appreciation for the man who brought us beautiful gadgets that changed the way we live. Jobs's genius also taught us brilliantly about innovation and passion, success, and failure.

Steve Jobs has always been a visionary genius. His passion for new products was contagious and inspired many people. He also made his greatest failure into his greatest success. We'll miss him.

Steve dropped out of Reed College after the first six months, but stayed around as a drop-in for another eighteen months before he finally quit. He slept on the floor in friends' rooms, returned Coke bottles for the nickel deposits to buy food, and walked seven miles across town every Sunday night to get one good meal a week at the Hare Krishna temple.

At that time, Reed College offered the best calligraphy instruction in the country. Throughout the campus, every poster and every label on every drawer, was written in beautiful calligraphy. Jobs found it fascinating and took a calligraphy class. Later, he used that knowledge in designing the Mac. It was the first computer with beautiful typography.

Steve Jobs was lucky that he found what he loved to do early in life. He and his partner, Steve Wozniak, started Apple Computer in his parents' garage when he was twenty. They worked hard, and in ten years, Apple had grown from the two of them in a garage into a $2 billion company with more than four thousand employees.

Jobs had just turned thirty when Apple released their finest creation, the Macintosh. A year later, Jobs was fired. How can one get fired from a company one started?

As Apple grew, Steve Jobs, who had no training in management, hired someone he thought was talented and experienced to run the company with him. The first year went well. However, soon their visions of the future began to diverge, and eventually they had a falling out. When the board of directors sided with the CEO, Jobs was fired. Whether the firing was justified or not is not important; he had learned a lesson and quitting was not an option.

He never gave up because he loved what he did. The turn of events at Apple did not change that. He had been rejected. He decided to start over.

During the next five years, he started a company named NeXT and another company named Pixar. Pixar created the world's first computer-animated feature film, Toy Story, and is now one of the most successful animation studios in the world.

In a remarkable turn of events, Apple bought NeXT with the help of Bill Gates from Microsoft. Steve Jobs returned to Apple, and the technology he developed at NeXT is at the heart of Apple's current Renaissance.

"Sometimes life hits you in the head with a brick," Jobs said. "Don't lose faith. I'm convinced that the only thing that kept me going was that I love what I do."

It's a shame that we lost Steve Jobs when he was only 56. His genius will truly be missed. Let us follow his advice:

Find what you love to do and go after it with a passion!

Many of you think you are only amateurs. You don't have the training or the degrees, your products are not yet perfected, you don't have the money, etc.

Remember Bill Gates, Steve Jobs, and Walt Disney were amateurs by the standards of the world. They were young men with dreams. They had no college degrees, but they dared to take action to support their vision and dreams with a passion and win against almost impossible odds.

God often used the insignificant to achieve the impossible.
—Dr. Robert H. Schuller

Amateurs with a passion built the ark.
Proud professionals built the unsinkable Titanic.
Passion makes all the difference.

Chapter 4

Excellent Financial Health

**Money is a wonderful slave, but a terrible master.
Make money work for you, but never be a slave for money.**

Everyone wants financial health. What is it? How can I improve my situation?

First and foremost, I want to point out again that "In a jungle, not only the lions eat." All the animals know that one does not have to be the strongest to survive and thrive in the abundance of the jungle.

For a good life, all we need are four basic ingredients:

1. Good clothing
2. Ample food
3. A comfortable home
4. Dependable transportation

If we have these four items throughout our lives, we are better off than 95 percent of the people on the earth and have enjoyed excellent financial health.

Unfortunately, according to a recent CNN report, "Currently, 49 percent of Americans have zilch savings for retirement." In this rich country of America, many people are living the good life on credit. When the slightest economic storm hits, they will lose everything.

In 1950, I came here as a broke foreign student who could hardly speak English. Today I humbly say that I've achieved a measure of the American dream, thanks to the grace of God, my many mentors, and the principles presented in this book. I'll share how the principles taught in this chapter can impact your life as it has mine.

I'll share with you some of the timeless truths about financial health and wealth generation from the book "The Richest Man in Babylon" by George S. Chasson. (Ref. 1, Appendix D)

In the ancient days of Babylon, wealth belonged to the well-heeled, noble class.

George S. Chasson's book presents a system from which ordinary people can learn and duplicate if they have the will and commitment to do so. Because of its importance, I've listed this particular book as our number one reference.

Truth is always simple.

The Seven Cures for a Lean Purse from the Richest Man in Babylon:

1. Start thy purse to fattening. (Raise your seed money.)
2. Control thy expenditures.
3. Make thy gold multiply.
4. Guard thy treasures from loss.
5. Make thy dwelling a profitable investment.
6. Insure a future income.
7. Increase thy ability to earn.

First Cure: Start thy Purse to Fattening (Raise seed money): the 10 percent (or 20 percent) solution

Make it a habit to take 10 percent out of your take-home pay and put it away before anything else. This will be your seed money for generating wealth in the future. Be sure your spouse supports you in your vision. You need a helpmate, not a dream killer. It requires sacrifice and discipline.

If you're a Christian, follow the John D Rockefeller's plan: take another 10 percent of your income as your tithe to the church, a joint covenant between you, your spouse, and God.

"I never would have been able to tithe the first million dollars I ever made if I had not tithed my first salary, which was $1.50 per week."— John D. Rockefeller

"Honor the Lord by giving Him the first part of your income, and He will fill your barns… to overflow!" Prov. 3:9-10

Build the Rainbow of Your Success

If you're one of the lucky few who received an inheritance, don't spend it. Put it away as your precious seed money.

Second Cure: Control thy Expenditures (Establish a Budget for the Remaining Money)

Set a budget carefully for the remainder of your take-home pay. Never spend more than that. Credit cards are ideal for shopping convenience and keeping records, but always pay them off at the end of each month. A credit card is a two-edged sword. It can help you, or it can kill you financially. This temptation of "easy money" has caused more personal financial failures than any other means. Credit card debt is the major cause of all personal bankruptcies in the United States. Never live beyond your means.

"Good planning and hard work lead to prosperity, but hasty shortcuts lead to poverty!" Proverbs 21:5

Third Cure: Make thy Gold (Money) Multiply

Deposit your seed money in an FDIC-insured savings account that pays a good interest rate. Here's an example: Suppose your monthly take-home pay is just $3,000. You want to create a nest egg by taking $300 and deposit it in a bank that pays an interest rate of X percent per year, compounded monthly.

Here's what will happen to your money:

Int. rate:	Year 1	Year 5	Years 10	Years 15	Years 20
5%/yr.	$3,784	$20,958	$47,855	$82,374	$126,675
3%/yr.	$3,708	$19,234	$41,410	$67,119	$96,922

This money will go a long way toward paying for your children's college education, the down payment on a home, or start a business.

Important! Note the big difference between 3 percent and 5 percent at the end of twenty years. Look for a financial institution with the highest interest rate consistent with the safety of your principal (FDIC insured). Imagine what would happen if you continued increasing your monthly savings as your income increased. . (Sorry that these interest rates have gone the way of low gasoline prices because of the current unsound fiscal policies, hopefully, it will be here again.)

Fourth Cure: Guard thy Treasures from Loss

One of the main reasons people lose their treasures is from greed. Instead of putting it in an FDIC-insured bank or a credit union that now insures the deposit up to $250,000, many people choose to follow some so-called guru's bad advice and go after risky investments they know nothing about, such as new company stocks, commodities futures, unsecured bonds, uninsured saving accounts, etc., hoping those investments will pay higher interest and bigger returns. Don't let anyone steal your nest egg! Keep your principal safe.

Beware of the coming hyperinflation and dollar devaluation. These are the two heads of the same economic monster. It's coming!

I experienced it in World War II in China. During that time, we were constantly running from the enemy. The Chinese paper currency was worthless; we called it "wet-wood," meaning it was not even good for burning. We survived on gold pieces and silver coins. Each child in our family wore a belt full of gold and silver coins as we ran as refugees. I still have childhood memories about wearing that heavy, uncomfortable belt; however, without it, I wouldn't be here writing this book now.

A case in point: When I came to America in the fifties, gold was selling at $32 per ounce. It has now gone up to almost $2,000 per ounce!

Fifth Cure: Make Thy Dwelling a Profitable Investment

According to the data from the Federal Reserve Board, across all groups, the 2007 median net worth was $120,300. Among them, a homeowner had $778,200; a renter or other had $70,600. Pay attention to this!

A great lesson was learned from my colleague's father.

In 1964, I came to California. I had a good job as a section head of a group of highly trained aerospace engineers and scientists. I purchased a house. I found a new 2,400-square-foot, tri-level, four-bedroom house in a new development project near my apartment. The price was $36,000 with a 20 percent down payment. I was excited.

Then I learned that an engineer, who worked for me, had bought a used, smaller, three-bedroom, 2,000-square-foot house in the Palos Verdes hills for $50,000.

Wow! "Why did you do that?" I asked.

"My dad told me," he said, "to buy a house in an area of future growth with a view and a good school system."

Four years later, when I sold my house to move to Orange County, my house had gone up to $42,000, only a $6,000 increase – not bad. But his house almost doubled in value! I learned a great lesson and am passing it on to you now.

Another colleague bought a beautiful home on a hill with a view overlooking Los Angeles. What he didn't know was that it had a school system with a very poor reputation. His son had to arrive an hour early to school so that the school bullies could copy his homework. Furthermore, his son had to bring extra lunch money to share with them or come home with a black eye. After one year, my colleague had to send his son to a private school with the tuition almost as much as his mortgage payments.

Having learned these lessons, we purchased our next 2,600-square-foot home in Irvine, next to the campus of one of the fastest developing universities of California. It cost $63,000 with a 20 percent down payment and a monthly payment of $300, a hefty sum of a professor's salary in 1970.

The house was on a hill, had more than 180-degree views, and was located in one of the best school systems in the state. Because we had a good financial plan (see seventh cure, below), we had no problem affording it. Eighteen years later, when I retired, I sold the house for more than **ten times** its original value.

Imagine what would have happened if I didn't buy the house, but had put the $12,600 down payment and the $300 house payment in the bank. At a 5 percent yearly interest rate, I would have built up a total saving of $137,047 in eighteen years, which isn't bad, but it's a far cry from $700,000 from the sale of the house.

Furthermore, if I didn't buy the house, my family and I wouldn't have been enjoying that beautiful home for eighteen years and all the rent money I would have had to pay would have been wasted.

Another advantage of home ownership is that most of your mortgage payments are interest and tax-deductible. Furthermore, the profit from the house sale years later will be considered a long-term capital gain and will be taxed at a much lower rate.

So listen to the "Richest Man in Babylon."
His advice is still right on.

Tips for purchasing your first home: If you're a young couple, don't head to your dream house right away. Be sure you can afford the payments with just one income. Many foreclosures happened when young people reached too high too soon and ran into trouble when the economic storm hit. Use the technique of trading up. Buy the first home you can afford, enjoy it, and as the equity and your income build up, trade up to the next home.

Q: When is a good time to buy a house? The answer is "any time is a good time." You are making a long-term investment. The market will go up and down, but it will always appreciate in the long run.

Important tips

1. **Never get variable-rate financing**, no matter how attractive the initial offer may appear to be. In the past, the interest rate has been known to have gone up to 15 percent per year, and your monthly payment would triple and you may lose your home.
2. **Always get a fixed-rate, thirty-year mortgage**. You should refinance whenever a lower fixed rate becomes available. For example: Take a $100,000 home with a thirty-year loan at 6 percent, your monthly payment is $599; if you can get a 3.75 percent loan later, your payment will be down to $463. The difference is $136. Add the $136 back to your new monthly payment (accelerated payment toward the principal), you pay the same payment as before ($599.) but you will pay off your loan eleven years sooner. Trust me; it works!

Sixth Cure: Insure a Future Income

Buy when everyone else is selling and hold until everyone else is buying.
—J. Paul Getty, industrialist

That's not just a catchy slogan. It's the essence of successful investing.

Once you own a home, your next project is to find a good investment to build a future income. For most people, rental properties are best.

According to the U.S. census data, the price of real properties increased on average by 5.4 percent annually from 1963 to 2008. Assuming that you put 20 percent down, and the rent covers your payments, taxes, and maintenance, your 20 percent down payment is actually enjoying more than 5x5.4%=27% appreciation yearly. Using the rule of 72, your investment (down payment) will double in just 2.67 years. Incredible!

In our case, we invested in a three-bedroom condo located right next to the eighteenth hole with a nice view of the golf course. In the seventies, it cost only $32,000 with 20 percent down. The complex contained a tennis court and a swimming pool. The place was beautiful and easy to rent. The rent payment covered all the costs and then some. In a few years, the price doubled. My neighbor, a realtor, brought in an offer for $69,000. In a weak moment, we accepted it.

It was a big mistake! The condo is worth more than $600,000 now after thirty years and would have been paid for with the rent money. What a nice nest egg it would have been! Furthermore, the net rental income alone is much better than my entire social security payment!

> So you see, I have not always been wise.
> ***Please don't repeat my mistakes.***

Upon reflection, I want to share these lessons:

1. Try to invest in a condo in a nice area, not a house unless you're very handy and can do the required

maintenance. Be sure to get a good security deposit to cover any damages.

2. Put enough of a down payment and get a fixed thirty-year mortgage so the rental income can cover all expenses with a slight surplus - a positive cash flow. Keep this surplus money in a savings account to cover vacancies and repairs. You should refinance whenever a lower fixed rate becomes available – lower your payments and increase your cash-flow.

3. Keep the rent slightly below the market so as to increase its demand. You can keep it rented easily and have the ability to select the tenants carefully from several applicants.

4. As the rents increase with time, the increasing small positive cash-flow and the value appreciation will be heaven sent.

Here is another important advice: if you are among the fortunate few that inherited a house free and clear from your parents, don't rush in and dump it on the market to cash out. The average house will double in value every 13.3 years, so hang on to it. If you need some cash for repair or investments, take a thirty-year mortgage out for the amount that an average rent can cover all the payments. Years later, you will be glad you follow this advice.

There are also many other forms of safe investments, so study them and choose wisely.

Seventh Cure: Increase Thy Ability to Earn

There are two types of incomes: **linear and leveraged income**.

In linear income, you exchange your time for money: a job. Leveraged income is earning money, using other people's time and money: a business.

When I moved to California in 1964, I had a good job. I could put away one week's paycheck into savings. I still remember the exact amount: $346 after tax. My plan called for doubling that amount. To do that, I had to get my bosses' job two to three levels up. That would take years.

I decided to invest in a small, part-time business that would generate another $400 per month. With my engineering and aircraft mechanic background, a self-service coin laundry seemed to be the best choice.

Upon investigation, I found that a new, fifty-machine store was available in a new Safeway shopping center at a nearby town. Because the store was bigger than average and the rent so high, the franchise owner had a hard time selling it. I was gutsy, naïve, or lucky and bought the store at a discounted price of $32,000 with $8,000 down and a payment of $650 per month for forty-eight months. As soon as I signed the papers, they turned over the keys. My adventure in business had begun. A lot of details waited to be solved, and they weren't easy ones.

Four Lessons I Learned in This Business

First lesson: Pray a lot! The franchise package included a grand-opening mailing campaign. I have to send out fifteen thousand mailers, offering up to four free washes to each family. At twenty-five cents per wash (in the sixties), my potential liability was $15,000!

Wait a minute! All these people in the neighborhood were poor; what if they filled out the form and put it in the box without doing any washing? The store was unattended, and no one would know, and I could go broke fast. We prayed a lot!

Surprisingly, at the end of the first month, we refunded exactly $748.25. The store broke even and was profitable from that day on. Amazingly, many refunds were only for twenty-five, fifty, or seventy-five cents. It's incredible that these people, though poor, had so much integrity. America has a future.

Second lesson: Give good people a second chance. Because it was a self-service coin laundry, I had to have someone clean the store, open, and close it each day. I had a problem.

Tim and his wife, a homeless couple, came in. Tim walked with a limp. They were a nice couple who had fallen into hard times. They lived in a small motor home, which they had to move nightly, always being chased out by the security guards.

They asked for a cleaning job. After finding out what they could do, I hired and paid them a living wage. They were overjoyed.

Someone asked me, "How could you trust them? They were homeless and had no résumé or reference."

"I don't look a gift horse in the mouth," I replied. "Live and let live. They looked like two typical buzzing bees; I wanted to give them a second chance in life."

As custodians of the place, they were allowed to park their motor home behind the store. They were not homeless anymore! They were honest and took care of the place as if it was their own. Because they lived behind the store, we kept the store open 24/7 without experiencing any major break-ins. A win-win situation.

Third lesson: Enjoy the appreciation and profits. After four years, I was offered a professorship at the University of California at the new campus in Irvine (UCI). We had to move fifty miles away to Orange County. We decided to sell the store. The price was $55,000. As the store was free and clear by then, my $8,000 investment went up seven times, not counting the monthly profits for four years.

Fourth lesson: Tax advantages. With a side business, you're entitled to the many tax advantages: your car mileage used for business, interests in your payments, equipment depreciation, and entertainments are typical examples. Many related expenses are write-offs against your current income. Furthermore, your profit from selling the business a few years later is considered a capital gain. (Your accountant will advise you, or you can Google it to find out more.)

Another Valuable Lesson I learned about Business

I almost lost one of the best investment opportunities by paying for bad advice.

Soon after my coin laundry business generated a positive cash flow, I came across an incredible franchise opportunity. In the sixties, cameras used color films. A new franchise called Fotomat was offered. The freestanding "island," installed in the parking lot of shopping centers, offered drive-through, twenty-four-hour film processing service. The franchise cost only $14,500. I jumped at the chance, put a $5,000 deposit to secure one of the top positions on the waiting list, and got the franchise agreement.

I came home all excited!

My wife said, "You what?" and insisted that I contact a lawyer friend to have him look over the agreement. He advised us that it was not a good agreement and rewrote it so it would be more equitable. I paid three hundred dollars for his advice. (Not a small sum in the sixties.)

When I presented the proposal to Fotomat, they quickly refunded my deposit. Their parting words were, "Bob, we like you, but as a franchisee, you must follow our system or nothing."

I was still intrigued with the idea and shared it with my office friends. One was interested. We formed a partnership and applied for a franchise again. Unfortunately, the franchise fee had risen to $19,000. We acquired it, and the deal was a big success. We recovered our original investment every year. After a few years—due to a dispute between the company and the franchisees—the company repurchased our store for $80,000, more than four times our initial investment. Incredible!

<u>Important lesson learned</u>: When seeking legal advice, find a specialist in the field. Our lawyer may not have been familiar with franchise laws. When starting a business, check with successful businessmen. Do not listen to the naysayers and busy bodies.

With the seed money from these two businesses, I was able to invest in many other businesses, such as other franchises, a commercial bank, a commuter airline, a bowling center and many real estate projects, etc.

All big rivers began with a trickle.

Caution: Don't rush out and buy coin laundries or any other franchises. Think and investigate before you leap. Each investment has its share of problems. Are you and your family ready for the challenges?

Blessings and success come from God! Always ask for guidance.

Important tip:

I always caution people concerning borrowing money for personal consumption, (i.e., credit card debts). However, do not hesitate to borrow money to buy your home or to start a business. Leverage is the name of the game!

Even if you have all the money needed, hold it in reserve; you may need it later.

Network Marketing: Another Possible Solution

If you have entrepreneurial tendencies and leadership skills, but don't have much money, network marketing is an excellent opportunity. Robert T. Kiyosaki, the author of the best-selling

Rich Dad Poor Dad, has written a book called "The Business School" (ref.4, appendix D) specifically for this purpose. It's an excellent reference. I have many friends who made six to seven figures per year in this industry within a few years in the business. This is a perfect example of leveraged income without requiring a lot of money.

Important Advice about Network Marketing

Never join a new start-up company. They always entice you by saying that you'll be the first one in, and everyone will be under you. What they don't tell you is that you may also be the first one to die with them. Don't fall for it. Here are the reasons:

1. Ninety (90) percent of most new US start-up companies fail within the first two years.
2. Among those that survive, ninety (90) percent will fail within the next five years.
3. Furthermore, never get talked into borrowing money to go into front-loading companies. (These companies require you to buy a lot of merchandise to be promoted to a higher position.) You may wind up with products you can't sell, and your friends won't talk to you anymore.

Don't be someone else's guinea pig. Investigate and be sure that the company has sound net worth, the product or products have real value, and the management has impeccable integrity.

My Experience with the Kangen Water ™ Opportunity

At the end of 2007, my wife was discharged from the City of Hope hospital after a nine-month bout with AML (Acute Myelogenous Leukemia). She was given a 2 to 5 percent of chance of survival. We were desperate in trying to find something that could help her.

Fortunately, we found Kangen Water produced by the Enagic Company, a thirty-seven-year-old billion-dollar company from Japan. It was newly introduced to the United States. We found it very helpful for our health, and we bought the machine and drank the ionized alkaline water. By early 2009, my wife's immune system was strengthened, and her blood tested normal. (See more details in Chapter 9.)

We also introduced this machine to one of our good friends, a retired eighty-year-old MD in internal medicine who had many health issues. Besides having a bad case of gout, (He walks with a cane). He also had spots on his brain and liver. His doctor also wanted to give him kidney dialysis!

He told me that, as an MD, he knew that if he took all those treatments, he would have no life! He was going to refuse all treatments and just wanted to give up and go home upstairs. I told him to try this water and gave him free water samples for a month.

His gout went away quickly (no more cane)! His spots went away and also experienced many health benefits. He bought the machine. He went out and shared the water with all of his friends and former patients. He sold more than a hundred machines! We kept getting thousands of dollars' worth of checks in our mailbox. We woke up and found out that this is a direct sales program with a very generous override system. *Their unique "compensation plan" is actually patented.* We started sharing the water with our friends and started enjoying a very good steady leveraged income. So if you are an entrepreneur and want to earn six figures or more a year part-time, check this out. Just go to my websites: www.vibrant-health-solutions.com Take the tour and get a free e-book.

In building a side business, always keep this in mind,

> a bold, greedy rabbit becomes a nice meal,
> a fearful rabbit starves in its hole,
> but a cautious rabbit thrives and multiplies.

As you begin your quest for wealth, you'll run into many stressful problems. You must learn to manage your time and your life. Here are some important lessons I learned.

On Time Management

When I returned to MIT for my doctorate, I was very nervous during my first exam. I had been out of school for five years and had forgotten how to take exams. I spent thirty minutes out of an hour-long exam looking at my watch. As a result, I finished one problem and barely had time for the four remaining problems. Fortunately, an understanding teacher gave me another chance.

After that, I learned the following principles of time management:

1. Begin each day by writing down a "do list."
2. Rank your problems from easiest to hardest.
3. Do the easy ones first and leave the hard ones until last.

4. After you have the easy ones under your belt, you'll have plenty of time for the harder ones.

An interesting observation: After you look through the problems and put the hard ones aside, your subconscious mind is already working on it while you solve the easy ones. When you're ready to tackle the hard one, the solutions may be already at hand.

Why? The power of your subconscious mind is always working.

This is the reason many Christians commit their problems in prayers at night. Sometimes God will inspire you through your subconscious mind while you sleep. Always have a pen and a notebook handy by your bed to write down the fresh inspirations. If you own a voice recorder, it's even better; you don't have to turn on the light.

On Life Management

When you start your ventures, you'll feel pressure from all sides. It's important to learn to handle them well.

I learned an important secret after I became a Christian. When I face a tough problem, I draw a vertical line on a paper. On one side, I write "God's problem." On the other side, I write "My problem."

God's problem	My problem

For example, you will have to give a presentation in the next town tomorrow. It's raining hard. The traffic will be bad going to the airport; they may even cancel the flight. What do you do?

The airplane and the weather are God's problem. You can do nothing about them, no matter how much you worry. On the other hand, are you well prepared for your talk? Is the computer, slides and projector in good order? That's your problem. So use your time and energy wisely to review your notes. Keep calm. To be safe, leave an hour early.

Anxiety comes when you try to solve God's problem.

bān	**mio**	**zh**	**zhǎng**
扳	苗	助	长

Don't pull on the rice to help it grow!
—A Chinese Proverb

Learn the lesson from the Chinese rice farmer. He carefully prepares the soil, floods the field, plants the tender seedlings in the wet soil, and waits for God to give the increase.

This Chinese proverb came from the story about an impatient boy who pulled the seedlings to make them grow faster and killed them.

So, remember this: Always do your best; let God do the rest.

Always remember yesterday is history.
You can learn from it but can't change it.
Tomorrow is a mystery and it is in God's hands.
Today is a gift from God, so take charge and enjoy today.

A Ballad of Wealth

The Lee family operated a small tofu (bean curd) shop in China and lived at the back of the store. They rose early each day and made a fresh, large batch of tofu. People loved their fresh product, and they always sold out by noon and closed the store. The husband then took out his Chinese stringed instrument and played it as he and his wife sang Chinese opera together. They were very happy.

Next to their shop was a large, successful department store owned by the Cheng family. They opened early and closed late at night and were doing well financially. However, the couple argued constantly because there was so much to do.

One day the wife complained to her husband, saying, "Why can't we be happy like the Lees?"

The husband shook his head and walked away.

The next day the music stopped, and this went on for several days. Mrs. Cheng wondered why. Her husband told her he had loaned a bag of money to the Lees and told them to expand their store and make more money.

A week later, the Lees returned the money, thanked them, and told the Chengs they were happy where they were.

Their music started again.

Wealth is not his who has it, but his who enjoys it.
—Ben Franklin

"If God gives us wealth and property, let us enjoy them…
It is a gift of God!"
Ecclesiastes 5"

Chapter 5

Our Vibrant Health

You Live in a Miracle Machine; Treasure It!

**Without health, we only endure life;
with good health, we enjoy our vibrant life.**

The Lunatic Driver

What would you say if you knew a driver who drove down the road with one foot hard on the gas and the other hard on the brakes all at the same time?

"He's a lunatic!" you would say.

The other day I ate lunch in a restaurant. The couple at the next table enjoyed thedouble cheeseburgers. The man finished with a slice of apple pie a la mode and helped his wife with her leftover cheesecake. He chased it down with a diet soda, probably thinking the drink was healthy by avoiding the nine teaspoons of sugar that comes in a regular soda. Before he left the table, he popped a handful of pills in his mouth.

As he lifted his three-hundred-pound-plus pear-shaped body from the table, I knew he was speeding down the freeway at full throttle toward diabetes, acid reflux, high blood pressure, heart problems, and many degenerative diseases, including cancer.

He is speeding down the highway toward ill health at full throttle by eating unhealthy food and drinking the wrong drinks. Then he hit the brakes hard, trying to stop the bad health symptoms with medicines and suffered the accompanying side effects. (Read the labels.)

While this metaphor may seem extreme, we can relate to it. Our bodies are a consequence machine. We can burn it up like the lunatic driver, drive it over a cliff, or navigate it to the road of good health and longevity. We all have a choice.

Here are important statistics:

1. According to the data from the World Health Organization (W.H.O.), the United States ranked thirty-seventh among nations on health care. Yet we are first on health care expenditures per capita.

2. According to Wikipedia, the United States ranked thirty-eighth in longevity, right below Cuba! Japan is ranked number one.

The important approach to good health lies in good eating and drinking habits. In other words, <u>good, vibrant health is based on nutrition and prevention, not medicine.</u> We must make the right choices in our daily living.

How the Body Works

In 2006, my wife was diagnosed with Acute Myelogenas Leukemia (AML), a dreadful blood cancer that required intermittent, strong chemotherapy treatments on and off for more than nine months. Fortunately, she's in complete remission now.

As her sole caretaker, I stayed by her bedside during most of her terrible ordeal. I experienced firsthand that:

Without health, nothing matters!

Lying on the hospital bed, not only the patient suffers, the whole family is devastated as well.

Whenever possible, I studied and researched our bodies, trying to understand how they function and the causes of such dreadful diseases. The first thing I found was that everything I learned in biology in China sixty years ago was obsolete.

You Are Wrong, Mrs. Wu

Mrs. Wu's biology class in the mid-forties in China was famous in our high schoolShe made the students come to the front of the class to discuss the human reproduction process.

She showed us the cutaway drawings of the human male and female reproductive system. We had to identify each part and explain how they functioned in the reproduction process. We were all very embarrassed, especially the girls. Mrs. Wu wanted us to know the sperm fertilized the egg in the uterus, where it grew for nine months. Then a baby was born.

With the invention of modern tools, such as the scanning electron microscope, computed tomography, the endoscopes, etc., modern microbiology has allowed us to look into the cells down to a few hundred nanometers. They've now shown us that conception actually occurs in one of the Fallopian tubes. Once fertilized, the cells start dividing, travel to the uterus, and take root on the uterine wall.

Was Mrs. Wu wrong? No. She was telling us what science had discovered in her time. Like Aristotle, who thought that the heart controls our emotions, our understanding must change as knowledge increases. A scientist's duty is to strive to gain new knowledge and continue learning. No matter where we are, more mysteries are waiting to be solved.

We all Started Life as a Big Winner

Amazingly, we all start life as a big winner in a great race with a field of up to five hundred million participants. In a sex act, up to five hundred million sperm cells are injected into the female. Only a few million make it to the uterus, and fewer still (five hundred) makes it to the Fallopian tube. All are racing toward the waiting ovum at roughly one inch per minute. We're the only ones who won.

Once the sperm penetrates the ovum's outer cover, the ovum releases a chemical that effectively shuts the door to other sperm. The fertilized ovum then splits and divides.

At first, the cells split and divide quickly; then, they slow down as the fetus grows. If the cells split just once a day, in nine months the number of cells will grow to 1.89 with eighty-one zeros behind it. We would literally explode from the mother's womb. Fortunately, the cell splitting slows down and follows a precise roadmap of development. Even with the modern knowledge of DNA and genomes, exactly how and why is still a mystery.

The Sea Urchin Experiment

Many years ago, an experiment was performed on a fertilized sea urchin egg by dividing and isolating the two cells shortly after its splitting process. The scientists fully expected the two separate cells to develop into two halves of a sea urchin when they were isolated from each other. Surprisingly, they both developed into identical, complete creatures.

Similarly, identical human twins were found to have developed from a single fertilized egg. How they became divided and grew separately into two identical babies sharing the same genetic endowment is still a mystery.

Another interesting discovery adds to the reproduction puzzle. For optimum sperm production, the male testes should be kept four degrees below the normal body temperature. Our body was designed to cool them by having them hang outside the body in the scrotum. It's believed that prolonged soaking in a 105-degree hot tub and wearing jockey shorts may reduce the quality and quantity of sperm production. A word to the wise is sufficient.

The Reproduction Paradox

In 1859, Charles Darwin wrote the Origin of the Species after observing the orderly progression of living things. His principles of evolution were based on "natural selection" and "survival of the fittest."

Later we discovered in the physical sciences that all matter is made up of atoms, electrons, and molecules. Electrons go around and around, but that's not life.

Then we discovered cells. A cell splits and reproduces itself. Ha, we call that life!

After that, we discovered DNA and genes, which provide the precise roadmaps for building different species and the various organs that work within each species of complex life forms.

Evolution is now being explained as the mutation of the genes following the principles of "natural selection" and "survival of the fittest."

It seems reasonable to assume that perpetuation of the species should be the prime directive for evolution. After studying the complexity of the human reproductive process, one wonders why, at the top of the evolutionary chain, we naturally selected such a difficult path for reproduction. If we evolved from lower animals, why is our reproduction process so complicated while theirs seem straightforward?

Take a dog, for example. When a female dog is in heat, sexual intercourse always produces a litter of puppies. The birth process for the dog is relatively simple. It doesn't appear to be painful, and no outside help is needed.

For human beings, however, it's a different story. First of all, in a sex act, only <u>one</u> out of up to 500 million sperm succeeds in fertilizing the egg, if at all. We also know that identical twins happened occasionally; coming from the same fertilized egg. The exact splitting process is not well understood. One wonders why evolution didn't naturally select the same splitting process and repeat it several times to produce a litter of babies, and then let "natural selection" and "survival of the fittest" take its course.

Two More Observations

The human baby is born with a hole in the heart, which originally enables it to take nutrients from the mother in the womb. This hole becomes a liability outside the womb. Fortunately, this hole is mysteriously and automatically plugged at birth; otherwise, the heart leaks, and the baby doesn't survive. (That's why infant open-heart surgery happens occasionally.)

The baby's lungs are full of fluids prior to birth. These fluids are quickly drained, unassisted, at birth, so the lungs can take in air. These two critical events are necessary for the baby's survival. Would our species have survived while waiting for thousands or millions of years for evolution to figure this out?

The Human Body: An Overview

When one examines the human body and sees the complex intricacy of this miracle machine that's made with roughly seventy-five percent water and about five dollars' worth of chemicals, one soon runs out of superlatives. "Amazing, incredible, and unbelievable" are not enough.

Being a space scientist for the past sixty years, I've worked on missiles, satellites, large launch vehicles, computers, and other complex machines. However, when we compare our accomplishments with that of the human body, our human accomplishments pale in comparison.

We live in a wonderful machine with amazing features that we should learn to truly appreciate, treasure, and not abuse.

From the beginning, we start with a single, fertilized cell. Nine months later, we've grown to trillions of cells. Furthermore, the cells have become specialized in functions and are grouped as tissues, organs, and systems.

There are hundreds of different cell types that produce more than fifty thousand different proteins to control how the cells work. For example, these include collagen to build skin, insulin to control energy use, and hemoglobin that greatly increases the ability of the red blood cells to carry and supply oxygen. Amazingly, these cells work and build together, following a fixed schedule and precise instructions to help prepare us for survival in the new environment at and after birth.

There are up to 100 trillion or more cells in an adult human body. Each cell has a structure and a job to do. They live, reproduce, and die. Each cell takes on nutrition and delivers its products. It's like a factory that produces a specific product. The human body is like a well-run country with 100 trillion inhabitants. (In comparison, the world has only 6.6 billion human inhabitants.) They live in utopia, and each does its specific job and obeys a central government (the brain).

The body has a transportation system (the blood) that delivers the nutrients and picks up the products from each cell and delivers them to be used in the various organs. The blood also carries out the waste products.

The body has a police department (the immune system), which keeps foreign matters out and cleans up the dead cells.

The body has an effective communication system (the nervous system), a complex sensory system, a digestive system, a reproductive system, etc., all controlled by the brain.

The Brain: the Incredible Central processor

1. It controls body temperature, blood pressure, heart rate, and breathing.

2. It processes a flood of information about the world around you from your various senses (eyes, ears, nose, skin, etc.) constantly and instantly.

3. It coordinates all physical motions when walking, talking, standing, or sitting.

4. It lets you experience emotions.

5. It also helps you think, dream, and reason.

All of these tasks are coordinated, controlled, and regulated by a cauliflower-sized organ: your brain, weighing about three pounds.

Brains have the following parts:

1. Brainstem: This controls the reflexes and automatic functions (heart rate, blood pressure), limb movements, and visceral functions (digestion and urination).

2. Cerebellum: The cerebellum integrates information from the vestibular system that indicates position and movement and uses this information to coordinate limb movements.

3. Hypothalamus and pituitary gland: These control visceral functions, body temperature, and behavioral responses such as feeding, drinking, sexual response, aggression, and pleasure.

The brain and the nervous system contain billions of neurons. Through the electron microscope and other means, we can see how the neuron works.

Through chemical stimulation, the neuron fires an electrical pulse that, in turn, causes other neurons to fire. After firing, the neuron returns to its original state similar to "0" and "1" in a digital computer. Amazingly, the neurons are not actually hardwired to each other (like that in electronics); in fact, they don't seem connected directly to anything. A small gap lies between the neurons; the signal is transferred more like dominos than direct connections.

Consider a mosquito sting. We sensed the pain from the intruder on the skin; neurons fire, traveling up the nervous system. The brain detects the exact position of the bite and orders the arm and hand to make a coordinated move to strike the mosquito. All these happen in a fraction of a second, even with our eyes closed. How the brain does this is simply amazing.

Another interesting fact: nerve endings lie in every part of the skin, up to 1,300 per square inch. When a cell fires, it's amazing how the brain knows precisely where the signal is coming from. We know which part of the brain works with these signals, but how it does it is a mystery. Furthermore, the same set of nerves can communicate pressure, pain, and heat, which require immediate responses, while it also senses caresses that are considered a pleasurable sensation.

Functionally, we've learned the brain can be trained to react quicker with practice. For example, kung fu masters teach their students to practice and practice until all movements are automatic, without conscious thought. This is also true with musicians. They don't consciously think about the notes. After a while, the music just flows. Similarly, most men thought about becoming gun fighters when they were kids. Assuming that the bullet travels at two thousand feet per second and the target stands thirty feet away, the winner must practice until he can draw and fire fifteen milliseconds (0.015 second) faster. That way the bullet will hit before the opponent can fire. Of course, accuracy is important; otherwise, he may be faster, but dead by natural selection.

The Human Transportation System: The Blood

Our blood contains four major parts:

1. Red blood cells: They carry oxygen (O_2) from the lungs to the body cells and carbon dioxide (CO_2) from the body cells back to the lungs to be exhaled.
2. Platelets: These clots the blood.
3. White blood cells: These fight germs that infect the body.
4. Plasma: A yellowish liquid consists mostly of water and nutrients.

Each drop of blood contains approximately five million red blood cells and five thousand white blood cells. Blood cells are produced in bone marrow. The average life of a red blood cell is about one hundred days. Every day billions of our red blood cells die and are replaced quickly by the bone marrow.

A red blood cell doesn't have a nucleus and doesn't reproduce or duplicate itself. Each red blood cell works like a small pickup truck that constantly delivers oxygen to the remotest cells and carries out the waste products. We have sixty thousand miles of blood vessels, twenty times the distance from coast to coast in the United States.

Our ten-ounce heart pumps seventy beats or more per minute, moving ten pints of blood through the circulatory system roughly one thousand times every twenty-four hours. The heart beats over a hundred thousand beats every day, 37 million beats per annum, and three billion times for an average lifetime. The mean time between failures (MTBF) is just incredible! Even more incredible is that the damaged or dead heart cells are constantly being replaced by new ones while the heart is busy pumping.

Scientific Facts

The red blood cell has a doughnut shape, but without the hole. Mathematically, it's proven to be the optimal shape for maximizing the surface area for a given volume. This shape is ideal for the red blood cell whose job is to absorb the oxygen quickly and deliver it to the cells in exchange for the carbon dioxide and waste. We learned these facts in freshman calculus. However, since a red blood cell has no nucleus and doesn't reproduce itself, how it evolves into this optimum shape is a mystery.

Fight or Flight?

In emergency situations, messages must be sent to all cells and organs. It's natural to assume that this task will be given to the nervous system. However, the nervous system isn't connected to every cell.

This job was actually given to the blood. The messages are carried by the blood, carrying a chemical "adrenaline" that stimulates various target cells. As a result, the heart responds by pumping harder and faster. The lungs let in more air, the liver releases more stored food for energy, and the blood flow from the gut and skin are diverted to the muscles. All this happens in an instant.

Adrenaline is one of the hormones produced by the glands and is controlled by the brain. There are many other hormones produced by various organs. They're released in short bursts in proper levels by a complex feedback system, the endocrine system. How the brain does this job continuously is yet to be discovered.

Our Police Department: The Immune System

Our immune systems defend us against a wide range of threats to our health. It acts like an organized army that protects us from diseases. The immune system consists of an array of organs, tissues, cells, and substances working together to protect us from the invasion of foreign materials: viruses, bacteria, pollen, cancer cells, etc. These cells are identified, attacked, destroyed, and literally eaten by this system.

The human immune system is complex. A brief overview of how it works follows.

Skin is the first wall of protection against foreign invaders. These invaders are trapped on the skin (actually a layer of dead skin) and can be removed by scratching or washing in daily showers.

The second line of defense is the mucus found in the respiratory system and tears from the eyes. These traps the invaders; and we expel them by sneezing, coughing, or blowing our noses. If the invaders pass through these defenses, there is another defensive line.

White blood cells have many weapons that fight germs and kill the invaders of the body, such as cancer cells.

White blood cells contain the following parts:

1. Helper T-cell acts as the "lookout" for the body by recognizing the invaders, then sending signals to the other white blood cells.

2. B-cells make antibodies to smother the invaders once they receive the signals from the helper T-cells.

3. Killer T-cells kill the invaders once they receive the signals from the helper T- cells.

4. Phagocytes act as "eating" cells. They destroy invaders with chemicals and then actually eat them.

The human immune system contains approximately one trillion T-cells and one trillion B-cells located in the lymphoid organs and in the blood, plus roughly ten billion antigen-presenting cells located in these organs. To maximize the chances of encountering antigens wherever they invade the body, lymphocytes continually circulate between the blood and certain lymphoid tissues. A given lymphocyte spends an average of thirty minutes per day in the blood, and, like a police officer on patrol, it recirculates about fifty times per day between the blood and lymphoid tissues.

Our immune system has three unique capabilities:

Recognition: It can identify "self" and "non-self"; otherwise, we destroy ourselves. It is like the police attacking ordinary citizens instead of the criminals.

Specificity: Once the "non-self" is identified, it calls for the most efficient defense against that specific invader. Vaccinations work by introducing weakened or killed viruses into the body to train the immune system and increase its effectiveness against that type of virus.

Memory: Once the immune system has destroyed a specific invader, it adapts and is more efficient in defending against it the second time around. This memory is the reason vaccinations work.

Disorders of the immune system can cause diseases.

Immunodeficiency diseases occur when the immune system is less active than normal, resulting in recurring and life-threatening infections.

Autoimmune diseases result from a hyperactive immune system that attacks normal tissues as if they were foreign organisms, a failure of "recognition". Common autoimmune diseases include rheumatoid arthritis, diabetes mellitus type 1, and lupus erythematosus. The critical role of immunology in human health and disease is areas of intense scientific study now.

Our Five Senses

We perceive the external world through our five senses: sight, hearing, smell, taste, and touch. When we examine our five sensing mechanisms, we are in awe of their wonderful designs and functions.

However, the more we study the animal kingdom, the more we realize our physical world is very small in comparison. .

1. The human eye can see only a narrow range of light, of wavelengths between red 750 NM (nanometer or one thousandth of a micrometer) and violet 380 NM, while a butterfly can sense down to 10 NM, and a viper can sense from 10 to 10,000 NM.

2. The human ear can hear sound waves between 20 to 20,000 hertz (cycles per second), while a bat can hear up to 200,000 hertz, and a pigeon can hear down to 0 hertz.

3. We can detect and recognize ten thousand or more different smells, which is remarkable. However, while we've 16 million olfactory cells, dogs and rabbits have over 100 million.

4. We have about nine thousand taste buds while a cow has twenty-five thousand.

5. Skin is only 1/20th of an inch thick, and yet it has up to 1,300 nerve endings. These nerve endings are sensitive to heat, cold, contact, pressure, and pain. Our fingertips are almost twice as sensitive as normal skin. Since it's very difficult to measure the sense of touch in animals, it's hard to make any direct comparisons.

Sometimes we wonder why we, the top of the so-called "evolutionary chain", have to give up so many capabilities as we evolved. Some say that we would have to have much bigger brains to handle that much more information. What limits our brains to three pounds anyway?

How We Age and Die

Recent studies show that while the body grows rapidly at birth, we stop growing by age twenty years. Cell division, called mitosis, creates more than 200 million cells in our bodies every minute. Some skin cells live only eight hours; the cells that line our intestines last only one and a half days. Liver cells live up to five hundred days. Many nerve and brain cells live as long as we do. Once they die, they're often not replaced.

Recent research showed some promise in replacing damaged brain cells in animals. There is hope.

Thus, the body is constantly renewing itself. Cells from a fetus double about fifty times before dying. As we grow older, this process slows. For an old person, the cells double only two to ten times before dying. Many cells die and are not replaced. That's why we shrink and wrinkle as we grow old.

Our brain loses cells at the rate of fifty thousand per day by the age of thirty, and many of these are not replaced. Recent findings show this rate of loss increases with alcohol and drug abuse and thus cause further loss of mental capacity. Interestingly, current research showed that this rate of loss may be slowed with better hydration and nutrition.

As many nerve and brain cells die and are not replaced, modern medical science is trying to find a way to create nerve replacement cells. The problem is not the creation of the cells, but how to place them so the connections are intact. Science fiction speculates that we can clone our own brain and have a brain transplant when we get old. The question is what would we be? Would we be just a mindless, soulless baby living in an old body? Would we want to live that way?

Acknowledgements: The information about the body was gathered from several sources, among them are: (1) The Incredible Machine by National Geographic Society; (2) The Human Body—An Overview by Mary Kittredge;(3) The Human Body—Explained by Philip Whitfield; (4) Intimate Universe, a video series by Robert Winston; and (5) The Cell, A Small Wonder, The Human Body Series, by Torstar Books Inc. (6) and researches through the Internet.

Interesting observations:

While my wife was in the hospital, I observed how Christians and atheists handled sickness and death. These observations are collaborated by nurses and chaplains.

Most Christians have peace while suffering; they're helpless but not hopeless. Indeed, if a Christian lives by the words of faith in the Bible, when he comes to the end of his life, he'll have love around him, peace within him, and hope, yes, hope still before him. That's why, in the final stage, many depart in peace with a smile.

For many atheists, the story is quite different. They tend to be irritable and constantly complaining, blaming the nurses and someone else for their misery. At death, they reach a crisis since they fear the unknown and lack peace. Many cried out to the unknown God in their desperation.

Taking Care of the Aging Body

As a consequence of the advancement of modern medicine and health care systems, our life expectancy in the United States continues to increase yearly. Presently it's about 78.2 years. Surprisingly, we rank only number thirty-eight in life expectancy in the world. Based on data from Wikipedia, Japan is ranked number one at 82.6 years. Modern research has shown that we can help ourselves prolong our lives by watching the food we eat and the water we drink. These actions can slow down general cell depletions and reduce the chance of failure of our major organs, as well as diseases such as cancer.

Primary Causes of Death

Cancer

Cancer is fast becoming the leading cause of death in the United States, taking over from heart disease in 2010. It's also the major contributor to the rising cost of health care.

Below are facts about this dreaded disease. According to the U.S. National Cancer Institute, in America alone:

1. More than 1.2 million Americans develop cancer every year.

2. A new cancer is diagnosed every thirty seconds.

3. One in two men will be diagnosed with cancer in their lifetimes.

4. One in three women will be diagnosed with cancer in their lifetimes.

5. Approximately eight thousand children will be diagnosed with cancer this year.

6. Cancer is the first cause of death in children between the ages of one and fourteen.

7. More than 565,000 Americans die from cancer every year.

Wow! <u>One out of two men and one out of three women will get cancer in his or her lifetime.</u> This is alarming. As both my wife and I are cancer survivors, I share with you what we've learned.

The life you save may be your own.

What Is Cancer?

Cancer is a group of more than one hundred separate diseases. These are characterized by an abnormal and unregulated growth of cells. This growth overwhelms and/or bypasses the immune system and destroys surrounding body tissue. It may spread to other parts of the body in a process known as metastasis.

Metastasis is the most frightening aspect about cancer. Metastasis is the process where millions of malignant cells release from the tumor (the primary) into the bloodstream. Fortunately, most of these cells are killed by the trauma produced while traveling within the blood vessel walls or by circulating white cells from the immune system.

Unlike infectious diseases such as AIDS, flu (influenza), or tuberculosis, cancer is not contagious; cancer is usually caused by genetic damage that happens inside an individual cell. The cells affected by cancer are called malignant cells. These are different from normal cells in that they divide (in most cases) more rapidly than normal cells. This is important to know because many drugs used to fight cancer attack malignant cells during the active phase of cell division. You may know someone who has had cancer, and his or her hair fell out during treatment. That happened because the anticancer drug(s) affected the normal hair follicle cells, which also divide rapidly, like that of the rapidly dividing malignant cells.

One Prime Origin and Cause of Cancer

Dr. Otto Warburg received the Nobel Prize in 1931 for his work in understanding "the nature and mode of action of the respiratory enzyme." He investigated the metabolism of tumors and the respiration of cells, particularly cancer cells. Dr. Warburg was director of the Kaiser Wilhelm Institute (now Max Planck Institute) for cell physiology at Berlin.

In his work, The Metabolism of Tumors, he hypothesized that all forms of cancer are characterized by two basic conditions: acidosis and hypoxia (lack of oxygen). Lack of oxygen and acidosis are two sides of the same coin; where you have one, you have the other.

"All normal cells have an absolute requirement for oxygen, but cancer cells can live without oxygen—a rule without exception." (Dr. Otto Warburg)

"Deprive a cell of 35 percent of its oxygen for forty-eight hours, and it may become cancerous." (Dr. Otto Warburg)

Dr. Warburg proposed that the prime cause of cancer is oxygen deficiency (brought about by toxemia). He discovered that cancer cells are anaerobic (don't breathe oxygen) and cannot survive in the presence of high levels of oxygen.

In 1966, Dr. Otto Warburg delivered a lecture at an annual meeting of Nobelists at Lindau, Germany. In his speech, he described the primal cause of cancer as follows:

"The prime cause of cancer is the replacement of the respiration of oxygen in normal body cells by a fermentation of sugar. All normal body cells meet their energy needs by respiration of oxygen, whereas cancer cells meet their energy needs in great part by fermentation. All normal body cells are thus obligate anaerobes, whereas all cancer cells are partial anaerobes. From the standpoint of the physics and chemistry of life, this difference between normal and cancer cells is so great that one can scarcely picture a greater difference. Oxygen gas, the donor of energy in plants and animals, is dethroned in the cancer cells and replaced by an energy-yielding reaction of the lowest living forms, a fermentation of glucose."

Cancer and Diabetes

According to US statistics, the baby boomers are reaching the age of fifty at the rate of ten thousand per day. Because of diet, most of these people are overweight and obese. As a consequence, many adult Americans have diabetes. If you're among this group, please heed this warning.

Dr. Warburg, winner of the 1931 Nobel Prize, discovered the following:

1. Cancer metabolizes differently than normal cells.

2. Normal cells need oxygen.

3. Cancer cells despise oxygen.

4. Cancer metabolizes through a process of fermentation of glucose; cancer loves sugar!

The metabolism of cancer cells is approximately eight times greater than the metabolism of normal cells. It's important to note that diabetes provides a futile (glucose-rich) field for cancer cells to grow.

Other studies also indicated diabetes doubles the risk of liver, pancreatic, and endometrial cancer. It increases the risk of colon, breast, and bladder cancer by 20 percent to 50 percent.

According to statistics from the United States National Cancer Institute, one in two men and one in three women will be diagnosed with cancer in their lifetimes. It's believed that this bias may be because more men are diabetics than women are.

Is Cancer Preventable?

Cancer is caused by a number of factors, some of which we can control and some we cannot. Certain cancers are associated with chromosomal abnormalities. Leukemia, sarcomas, lymphomas are typical examples. There are also viruses associated with cancer.

In their landmark 1981 study, Sir Richard Doll, a British physiologist, and Sir Richard Peto, an Oxford professor of medical statistics and epidemiology, set out to determine the causes of preventable cancer in the United States. According to Doll and Peto, pollution accounted for 2 percent of all cancer cases, and geophysical factors accounted for another 3 percent. They noted that 80 to 90 percent of cancers are caused by environmental factors. These included things such as smoking, diet, occupational exposure to chemicals, malnutrition, and geophysical factors. Geophysical factors include naturally occurring radiation, man-made radiation, medical drugs, and medical radiation. Tobacco use accounts for about 30 percent of all annual cancer deaths. Dietary choices account for 35 percent of annual cancer deaths.

Two professors from the University of California, Berkeley, Bruce Ames and Lois Swirsky Gold, have come to similar conclusions, noting that smoking causes about a third of all cancers. They underline the importance of diet by highlighting that the quarter of the population who eat the fewest fruits and vegetables double their cancer incidences versus those eating the most fruits and vegetables. They concluded that "there is no convincing evidence that synthetic chemical pollutants are important as a cause of human cancer."

Cancerous tissue, above other consequences of choice, has countless secondary causes. Modern research in medical sciences has determined the prime origin and cause of cancerous tissue is the over-acidification of the tissues. For women, breast cancer should be tested by self-examination every month for women over eighteen. Breast examination by a woman's doctor should be completed every three years for women between the ages of eighteen and forty, then every year after age forty. A mammogram should be taken between the age of thirty-five and forty as a baseline, then every one to two years between ages forty and forty-nine, then annually after age fifty. Women should also receive a Pap smear annually to screen for cervical cancer between the ages of eighteen and sixty-five. An evaluation of the pelvis to screen for cervical, uterine, and ovarian cancer should be performed every one to three years between the ages of eighteen and forty, then annually.

For men, screening for prostate cancer should be completed yearly after age fifty (forty-five for high-risk individuals), which includes rectal examination and a blood test for prostate-specific antigen (PSA). Screening for rectal and colon cancer should be done with an annual rectal examination after age forty, with stool examination annually after age fifty, and with colonoscopy every three-to-five years after age fifty.

Cure and Relapse

Most cancers can be controlled and be forced into remission, but never fully cured. Why? **<u>Cancer cells don't die naturally!</u>**

The 2009 Nobel Prize winner in medicine, Dr. Carol Greider, discovered that all cells age and die except cancer cells. **Cancer cells do not age!**

This is worth noting. Once cancer cells live in our bodies, they don't die naturally. Many cancer treatments, such as chemotherapy, can kill cancer cells as well as good cells, but often they do not succeed in killing all of them.

The remaining cancer cells live in our bodies like ticking time bombs. They must be searched out and killed by our immune systems. That's why cancer often relapses if the immune system is weak, likely weakened by chemotherapy. As a consequence, it may not be as effective in searching and destroying cancer cells. Uncontrolled growth of cancer cells causes relapse to occur. Unfortunately, when a cancer relapses, it often shows up in other parts of the body.

No Relapse

In a lecture on cancer delivered by Dr. Hiromi Shinya, inventor of the colonoscope (the Shinya method) and author of The Enzyme Factor, the following points were laid out:

1. Cancer is acidic and cannot survive in an alkaline environment.

2. Cancer cannot survive in a high oxygen environment.

3. If your immune system is strong, the cancer will not survive.

4. If your immune system is weak, the cancer will spread like time bombs exploding throughout the body.

All of his cancer patients (370,000+) who followed Shinya's recommended diet and drank Kangen Water - ionized alkaline water, kept their key enzymes from being depleted, their immune systems strong, and experienced no relapse!

Once you have cancer, NO RELAPSE is the magic phrase.

Dr. Hiromi Shinya is professor of surgery at Albert Einstein College of Medicine and head of the Endoscopy Center of Beth Israel Hospital in New York City. He's the author of the US bestseller, The Enzyme Factor, in which he presents his research, grounded in his forty-five years of medical practice in the United States and Japan. This research supports the idea of a miracle enzyme, out of which all the enzymes the body needs, is produced. He suggests cancer and other diseases occur when this key enzyme is depleted and can't do its job properly. In his book, he clearly shows how what we eat and drink affects that key. (Ref. 27, 28 Appendix D.)

Things We Can Do to Prevent Cancer

The cure for cancerous tissue is more likely to be found in cancer prevention than in its treatment. That prevention can only be obtained by making healthier lifestyle and dietary choices.

A cancerous condition is often the consequence of choice. For example, if you want to reduce your risk for cancer of the lungs, stop smoking and stop associating or working around people who smoke. Secondary smoke is as acidic and damaging to the lung tissue as primary smoke.

If you want to reduce your risk of getting a cancerous liver, stop drinking alcohol and carbonated drinks.

To reduce your risk of a cancerous pancreas, Dr. Shinya recommends you stop eating acidic foods, sugar, and soft drinks, including diet soft drinks (very acidic with a pH2.4).

Dr. Shinya recommends that to reduce the risk of a cancerous bowel, cut down on animal protein, and drink Kangen Water - ionized alkaline water. The micro-cluster and strong antioxidant properties of this water will keep your colon clean.

The former US Surgeon General, C. Everett Koop, said about diet: "Your choice of diet can influence your long-term health prospects more than any other action you might take." (For more information, go to: http://health.howstuffworks.com/cancer.htm and http://www.cancer.org and look for "Lifetime Probability of Developing or dying from Cancer.")

Heart Attack

Each year, more than a million persons in the United States have a heart attack. Approximately half (515,000) die and half of those die within one hour of the start of symptoms and before reaching the hospital.

A heart attack occurs when the blood and oxygen supply to an area of heart muscle is blocked, usually by a clot in a coronary artery, and may bring about sudden death. If the blockage isn't treated within a few hours, the affected heart muscle will die.

Heart Attack Warning Signs

Some heart attacks are sudden and intense. These signs can mean a heart attack is happening:

Chest discomfort: It can feel like uncomfortable pressure, squeezing, fullness, or pain. It often subsides and returns.

Discomfort in other upper body areas: Symptoms can include pain or discomfort in one or both arms, the back, neck, jaw, or stomach.

Shortness of breath: Can occur with or without chest discomfort.

Other signs: These can include breaking out in a cold sweat, nausea, or light- headedness.

Stroke Warning Signs

The American Stroke Association gives these stroke warning signs:

1. Sudden numbness or weakness of the face, arm, or leg, especially on one side of the body.
2. Sudden confusion, trouble speaking, or understanding.
3. Sudden trouble seeing in one or both eyes.
4. Sudden trouble walking, dizziness, loss of balance, coordination.
5. Sudden, severe headache with no known cause.

Pay Attention to This. It May Save Your Life!

A heart attack or stroke is an emergency. Call 9-1-1 if you think you (or someone else) may be having a heart attack or stroke. Emergency medical services (EMS) staff can begin treatment when they arrive up to an hour sooner than if someone drives the patient. Prompt action can save lives. (For more details, see http://www.americanheart.org/.)

How Substance Abuse Affects Our Bodies
Tobacco: The Silent Killer

According to US statistics in 2004, 44.5 million smoked cigarettes among adults. About 23 percent (one out of four) of men and 19 percent (one out of five) of women were smokers, even though cigarette smoking has declined from about 42 percent in 1965 to about 21 percent in 2004.

Tobacco use, including smoking cigarettes, chewing tobacco, and dipping snuff, remains common among American youth. According to the recent government surveys, more than one in four high school students (28 percent) used some type of tobacco in 2004, and more than one in five (22 percent) were considered current cigarette smokers. Cigar smoking was also common among high school students (about 14 percent).

Students, who smoke may be more likely to use other drugs, get into fights, carry weapons, attempt suicide, and engage in high-risk sexual behaviors.

Studies also show that cigarette smoking is most likely to become a habit during the teen years. Almost 90 percent of adult smokers became addicted to tobacco at or before eighteen.

How Does Tobacco Affect Health?

In large doses, nicotine is a poison and can kill by stopping a person's breathing. Because nicotine affects the chemistry of the brain and central nervous system, it can also affect the mood and nature of the smoker.

The smoke contains tar, which consists of more than four thousand chemicals, including more than sixty known to cause cancer. Some of these substances cause heart and lung diseases, and all can be deadly. Here are some examples:

- Cyanide
- Benzene
- Formaldehyde
- Methanol (wood alcohol)
- Acetylene (fuel used in welding torches)
- Ammonia

Cigarette smoke contains poisonous gases: nitrogen oxide and carbon monoxide. Modern research shows that the use of tobacco accounts for about one-third of all US cancer deaths. Smoking causes almost 90 percent of lung cancers. Smoking causes cancers of the larynx (voice box), oral cavity, pharynx (throat), esophagus, and bladder and contributes to the development of cancers of the pancreas, cervix, kidney, and stomach. It's also linked to the development of some leukemia. Cigars, pipes, and chewing tobacco all can cause cancer.

Modern research shows that smoking as few as one to four cigarettes a day can have serious health consequences, including an increased risk of heart disease and a higher risk of dying at an earlier age, even if from light cigarettes with lower tar and nicotine content, hand-rolled cigarettes, or all-natural cigarettes. Herbal cigarettes contain toxins, including tar and carbon monoxide.

The Dangers of Environmental Tobacco Smoke (ETS)

ETS, also known as passive smoking or secondhand smoke, occurs when nonsmokers inhale other people's tobacco smoke. Strong evidence shows ETS causes serious damage to human health. ETS causes about 3,400 lung cancer deaths and about 46,000 deaths from heart disease yearly in healthy nonsmokers who live with smokers.

Pregnant women exposed to ETS are at risk for having a baby with a low birth weight baby and may also experience preterm delivery and miscarriage.

Warning: There's no such thing as a safe smoke. The truth is smokers are not poisoning only themselves, but also their loved ones as well. (The author had personally lost a younger sister to lung cancer, due to second hand smoke.)

How Tobacco Use Affects the Economy

Some people believe the tobacco industry is one of the most profitable businesses in the country, making billions of dollars yearly, and is important to our economy. Recent studies show the cost of smoking is far higher than the income from cigarette sales.

Smoking causes more than $167 billion each year in health-related costs, including the cost of lost productivity due to smoking.

Smoking-related medical costs totaled more than $75 billion in 1998 and accounted for 8 percent of personal health care expenditures.

Death-related productivity losses, due to smoking among workers, cost the US economy more than $92 billion yearly (average of 1997–2001). For each pack of cigarettes sold in 1999, $3.45 was spent on medical care due to smoking, plus $3.73 in lost productivity, for a total cost of $7.18 per pack.

Tobacco use causes us to lose health as well as wealth.

For more information, see the American Cancer Society document, Guide to Quitting Smoking.

How Alcohol Affects the Body

All alcoholic drinks contain ethyl, a compound made up of carbon, hydrogen, and oxygen—C_2H_5OH, a toxin to the body.

After the consumption of one standard drink, the amount of alcohol in the drinker's blood peaks within thirty to forty-five minutes.(A standard drink is defined as twelve ounces of beer, six ounces of wine, or one and a half ounces of eighty-proof distilled spirits, all of which contain the same amount of alcohol.)

When an alcoholic beverage is consumed, it enters the bloodstream through the walls of the small intestine. Through oxidation in the liver, alcohol is detoxified and removed from the blood, preventing the alcohol from accumulating and destroying cells and organs. However, the liver can metabolize only a certain amount of alcohol per hour. Until all the alcohol consumed has been metabolized, it's distributed throughout the body, affecting the brain and other tissues.

Women absorb and metabolize alcohol differently than men. They have higher blood- alcohol concentrations (BAC) after consuming the same amount of alcohol as men and are more susceptible to alcoholic liver disease, heart muscle damage, and brain damage.

Alcohol acts as a drug affecting the central nervous system. Most people begin to show measurable mental impairment at around 0.05 percent blood alcohol. At around 0.10 percent mental impairment will show obvious physical signs, such as an unsteady walk and erratic driving. Slurred speech shows up at around 0.15 percent. Unconsciousness results by 0.4 percent. Above 0.5 percent, the breathing center of the brain or the beating action of the heart can be anesthetized, resulting in death. (Source: www.intox.com/about_alcohol.asp.)

Drug Abuse

Drug abuse falls into three categories: depressants (e.g., heroin or barbiturates), stimulants (e.g., cocaine, crack, or amphetamines), and hallucinogens (e.g., marijuana, ecstasy, or LSD). Drugs are usually ingested, inhaled, smoked, injected, or snorted.

Depressants are sedatives that act to slow down the activities of the nervous system. Stimulants are agents that activate, enhance, or increase activity of the central nervous system.

Stimulants can give rise to symptoms suggestive of intoxication, including tachycardia, pupillary dilation, elevated blood pressure, and nausea or vomiting. They can cause violent and aggressive behavior, agitation, and impaired judgment.

Hallucinogens are chemically diverse and produce profound mental changes such as euphoria, anxiety, sensory distortion, vivid hallucinations, delusion, paranoia, and depression. They include mescaline and LSD.

Drugs can be harmful in a number of ways, both through immediate effects and damage to health over time. LSD distorts perceptions, alters heart rate and blood pressure, and in the long-term causes neurological disorders, depression, anxiety, visual hallucinations, and flashbacks.

Cocaine and amphetamines cause tremors, headaches, hypertension, and increased heart rate. Long-term effects include nausea, insomnia, weight loss, convulsions, and depression. Heroin use initially results in nausea, slow respiration, dry skin, itching, and slow speech and reflexes. It can cause the development of physical and psychological dependence. An overdose can cause death due to respiratory depression.

No illicit drug can be considered safe. In one way or another, the use of drugs alters the normal functioning of the human body, and in the long run, they can cause serious harm.

Sexual Abuse

In our modern society, there's another way we can abuse our bodies. Movies and TV broadcasts are racing each other to export lust and temptations to the public. Many people who lack wisdom and understanding are falling into the trap and turning beautiful, sacred human sexual relationships into basic animal behavior. Mixed with alcohol and drugs, many people are like moths flying into the fire and ruin their lives physically and spiritually.

In the world, sexually transmitted diseases (STDs) are becoming significant public health concerns. More than twenty-five diseases are transmitted through sexual activity. Other than HIV, the most common STDs in the United States are chlamydia, gonorrhea, syphilis, genital herpes, human papillomavirus (HPV), hepatitis B, trichomoniasis, and bacterial vaginosis.

According to the Center of Disease Control (CDC), the only way to protect yourself totally against HPV is to avoid sexual activity that involves genital contact. There are approximately six million new cases of genital HPV in the United States every year; 74 percent occur in fifteen to twenty-four-year-olds.

Human Immunodeficiency Virus (HIV)

HIV is a retrovirus that can lead to acquired immunodeficiency syndrome (AIDS), leading to life-threatening infections. HIV infections can occur with the transfer of blood, semen, vaginal fluid, and worst of all, breast milk to infants.

As of January 2006, the Joint United Nations Programs for HIV/AIDS (UNAIDS) and the World Health Organization (WHO) estimate that AIDS has killed more than 25 million people since December 1, 1981, making it one of the most destructive pandemics in recorded history.

In 2005 alone, AIDS claimed an estimated 2.4 to 3.3 million lives, of which more than 570,000 were children. A third of these deaths occurred in Africa, retarding economic growth and increasing poverty. According to current estimates, HIV is set to infect 90 million people in Africa, resulting in a minimum estimate of 18 million orphans.

If you want a great future, don't abuse your sexual activity. Don't play this Russian roulette.

Food Abuse

In our modern society, food is plentiful and easily affordable. People are on the go and don't take enough time to eat properly. Because of the large profits associated with the marketing of fast and fatty foods, most advanced, civilized societies are faced with obesity in adults and children. In the United States, obesity is becoming a national epidemic. Every day four thousand American adults (1.5 million per annum) are diagnosed with type 2 diabetes, a direct result of obesity.

Food Abuse Affects Our pH Balance

As mentioned earlier, the body is comprised of about 75 percent water and chemicals that cost five dollars. How a human body works, grows, and maintains its health is still a mystery. The modern research objective is to uncover these mysteries, using our remarkable brains. One discovered fact is that health depends on balances. Our body has a built-in system to help us maintain proper balance so we can survive in a hostile environment.

For example, the body has an efficient temperature regulation system. It keeps our inner organs at a temperature of near 98.6 degrees Fahrenheit, so they can function properly. This process is one aspect of homeostasis: a dynamic state of equilibrium between our internal and external environments. When body temperature increases significantly above normal, a condition known as hyperthermia occurs. That's why so many poor, elderly persons die during a heat wave.

The opposite condition, when body temperature decreases below normal levels, is known as hypothermia. Fortunately, there are things we can do to help the body. For example, a lowly blanket can become a life-saving miracle if you're suffering from hypothermia.

Similarly, we have an efficient system to maintain the proper glucose level. However, if we eat the wrong foods and drink too many sodas (acidic, with pH 2.5), we'll become obese, eventually overstress the pancreas, and become a diabetic.

One of the most tightly regulated systems is the pH of blood. The ideal blood pH is 7.365. It can vary only a small amount and still keep the cells alive. In fact, when blood pH is lower than 7.2, cardiovascular complications can occur. Our body will do anything, even at the expense of our bones, organs, and other tissues, to keep the pH at the proper level.

We're polluting our bodies with too much acid-producing activities; among them smoking, drinking too much alcohol, and eating an excessive amount of acid-producing foods such as dairy products, sugar, animal protein, processed grains, junk food, and soda (pH 2.4).

Recent research found that although we blamed the fat from fast-food restaurants for making us fat, actually the unlimited soda fountain is the real cause. With a pH of 2.4 and loaded with sugar, drinking soda has caused us to become overly acidic. Do you know that an average schoolboy takes between thirty-four teaspoons of sugar a day with soda?

Studies also show that the consumption of soda will lower the bone density of children, as well as adults. Why? The body is using too many calcium reserves to balance the acidity. If we continue to abuse the body with highly acidic food and drinks, over time all these factors will add up to produce the toxic liquid called acidity, which causes our blood regulation systems to "rob Peter to pay Paul" and can cause our vital organs to shut down and our bones to become brittle. If this acidic state continues, the result is chronic disease, cancer, and even death.

Fortunately, this acidity can be reversed if we catch it in time. Just as a simple blanket can save one from hypothermia, eating more alkaline fruits and food and drinking ionized alkaline water can neutralize this acidity and revitalize our organs and our health.

Effects of Food Abuse on Health

Obesity is a major cause of cardiovascular disease, diabetes type 2, high blood pressure, acid reflux, high blood cholesterol, and high triglyceride levels. Recently it was discovered that obesity is a major cause of sleep apnea, which affects a person's mental and physical health as well as productivity. Studies also link sleep apnea to Alzheimer's and may cause other forms of brain deterioration. A severe case of sleep apnea is also a life-threatening condition.

Acid Reflux

Acid reflux is a common disease that seriously affects more than 20 to 25 percent of the US population. It's also known as Gastro Esophageal Reflex Disease (GERD). People of all ages and races, especially the baby Boomer generation, suffer with this painful ailment.

People often confuse acid reflux with burping. Burping is a symptom caused by eating too fast and swallowing too much air. Burping, in general, is annoying but not harmful.

Acid reflux is a different matter. Its primary symptoms are heartburn and chest pain radiating to neck, back, and shoulders. Choking, vomiting, difficulty in swallowing, and insomnia due to pain and burning sensations in the esophagus and chest are also common symptoms of this ailment. Furthermore, acid reflux is linked as a main cause of esophageal cancer.

The cause of acid reflux is mainly the regurgitation or refluxing of partly digested food (chyme) back to the esophagus.

One naturally assumes that it's due to hyperacidity and starts taking antacids and other stronger medicines (acid inhibitor or blocker). This will offer temporary relief, but in the long run, it will cause harm to the digestive system and affect other organs.

Dr. Shinya recommends we chew food fifty to seventy times before swallowing so that saliva and enzymes can do their jobs properly. We Americans lack the patience; we chew food ten to twenty times and wash it down with water, coffee, or tea. Indigestion and constipation are the direct consequences.(See Dr. Shinya's books, The Enzyme Factor. The Rejuvenation Enzyme. Ref. 27, 28)

Swallowed food is pushed into the esophagus, which connects the throat to the stomach. At the junction of the esophagus and stomach, a ring-like muscle called the lower esophageal sphincter (LES) closes the passage between the two organs. As food approaches the closed sphincter, the sphincter relaxes and allows the food to pass into the stomach. Once food has reached the stomach, the lid of the sphincter muscle closes like a one-way check-valve and prevents food from refluxing.

Once food reaches the stomach, digestive glands in the stomach lining produce strong acid (pH 1.4) and an enzyme that digests protein. A thick mucus layer coats the gastric mucosa and helps keep the acidic digestive juice from dissolving the tissue of the stomach. For most people, the stomach mucosa is able to resist the juice, although food and other tissues of the body cannot.

The stomach's exit is the duodenum. This is a hollow, jointed tube about 25 to 30 centimeters (10 to 12 inches) long, connecting the stomach to the small intestine. It curves down, then up from the pylorus of the stomach, where chyme enters the bowels. The ducts from the pancreas and gallbladder bring in bicarbonate to the duodenum to neutralize stomach acid, pancreatic enzymes to further digestion, and bile salts to break up fats.

The duodenum has an important job; it acts as a valve to prevent the acidic chyme to enter the small intestine until it is neutralized by the juices from the gall bladder and pancreas, to bring the pH up to 7.5 or 8. Otherwise the small intestine and all of its small, finger-like villi necessary for nutrient absorption would be destroyed by the acidic chyme.

The common belief is that acid reflux occurs when the (LES) sphincter muscle fails to close properly and allows the acidic chyme to back up.

Another culprit, the duodenum, is actually to blame. As we get older and overeat, our store of essential minerals runs low, and often the liver and pancreas cannot generate enough juices to neutralize the acidic chyme, and the duodenum will not let the chyme through. So the chyme churns in the stomach and some get past the LES and go up the esophagus. When it hits the airways, we choke!

So if you're experiencing acid reflux, before getting antacids and other medicines (with their side effects), below are suggestions for controlling it:

1. Because reflux is more likely to occur when you're lying down, allow at least three, preferably four, hours to pass between your evening meal and bedtime. During this interval, you may drink water, but nothing else. By allowing a few hours to pass after your evening meal, you give the stomach time to empty before you're horizontal.

2. Modify the character of your evening meal. If possible, make your noon meal your heavy meal, so you'll be content with a lighter evening meal. Avoid fried or other fatty foods, because fat stimulates the stomach to secrete acid and digestive enzymes.
3. Several substances are known to relax the LES. Caffeine, nicotine, chocolate, and mint are the main culprits. Avoid all these substances for at least four hours before bedtime. Alcohol is also a no-no.
4. Obesity contributes to the problem. If you're overweight, begin a sensible diet that includes smaller portions.
5. Elevate the head of your bed. The goal is to elevate your esophagus and throat above the level of your stomach, so gravity works in your favor. A tilt-up bed (like a hospital bed) works well.
6. Drink ionized, alkaline (Kangen) water regularly (six to eight cups per day). Surprisingly, the purpose of drinking this water is not to neutralize the chyme (it's not an antacid), but to help the body absorb and store more essential minerals. (i.e., calcium, magnesium, etc.; these elements are in Kangen water.) These minerals in turn help the liver and pancreas to produce more needed juices to neutralize the acid in the duodenum. Once the duodenum neutralizes the chyme, it empties the stomach. No more refluxes.

The Key to Health and Fitness

According to the latest data from the US Agency for Healthcare Research and Quality (AHRO), the ten most expensive health conditions are:

* Heart conditions, $76 billion
* Trauma disorders, $72 billion
* Cancer, $70 billion
* Mental disorders, including depression, $56 billion
* Asthma and chronic obstructive pulmonary disease, $54 billion
* High blood pressure, $42 billion
* Type 2 diabetes, $34 billion
* Osteoarthritis and other joint diseases, $34 billion
* Back problems, $32 billion

We have more medicine and health care than anywhere in the world; yet we rank number thirty-eight in overall health. The truth is that, as a nation, we need more education, not more medication.

Question: Is there anything we can do proactively to improve health and fitness? The answer is definitely yes. We can improve our lifestyles and exercise moderately.

Improving Our Lifestyles

Recently, a new book entitled The Enzyme Factor by Dr. Hiromi Shinya was published in the United States. This book was first published in Japan entitled How to Live Long and Never Get Sick, which sold over two million copies.

Dr. Shinya is the inventor of the Shinya Method (colonoscope) and practices gastroenterology in New York City and in Japan. He just retired as clinical professor of surgery at the Albert Einstein College of Medicine and chief of the Endoscopy Unit of the Beth-Israel Hospital in New York City.

In his book, Dr. Shinya points out that the body is alkaline by design but is made acidic by our lifestyles. This lifestyle depletes enzymes essential to health. He believes that if we follow his lifestyle recommendations, we may prevent many diseases.

Here's an unbelievable claim. Among his thousands of cancer patients, there has been no relapse of cancer among those who followed the Shinya diet and drank Kangen water, ionized alkaline water, as part of his health regimen. With his impeccable credentials as a preeminent gastroenterologist, I believe that what he claims merits serious consideration.

He is more than seventy years old. His findings and recommendations are based on more than forty years of his clinical practice (more than 375,000 patients). Besides avoiding alcohol, tobacco, drugs, and carcinogens, one must eat the proper foods, chew them well, and drink ionized alkaline water between meals.

We have personally followed Dr. Shinya's advice and experienced the benefits. The reason is simple and understandable. Our bodies are like a country with up to 100 trillion (cells) inhabitants, and each has a function. Our blood is 90.7 percent water and is the river of life. The red blood cells are like little pickup trucks that constantly deliver oxygen to our cells while the white blood cells keep us healthy. The blood also delivers nutrients and carries out products and waste products. Each cell lives and dies and is constantly being replaced. When the replacement lags behind, we age. The function of fresh, clean, alkaline water, which is needed in the body to hydrate, detoxify, and oxygenate, alkalizes the body's pH, enhances our immune systems, and is a good partner to our source enzyme. A properly functioning body is capable of healing itself. I recommend this book highly.

How to Care for Our Bodies: Exercise

We know intuitively that exercise improves health. However, recent statistics show that the life expectancy for the National Football League (NFL) players is just fifty-five; twenty-three years shorter than average. Too much exercise may not be good for you.

For the average person, how much exercise is enough?

Many middle-aged Americans rush into health clubs to lift weights and do aerobics and wind up having muscle aches and joint problems due to high impact. Worst of all, some suffer strokes and heart attacks.

On the other side of the globe, variations of tai chi ch'uan are being practiced every morning in parks across China. The traditional tai chi training is intended to exercise at both mental and physical levels. While many Chinese believe that tai chi is the road to health for the elderly, many Westerners wonder if it's effective since the practitioner seldom works up a sweat.

The following are excerpts from an article that may shed some light on this matter. It's entitled Exercise—No Pains, Big Gains, published on the Internet (www.intelihealth.com) by Dr. Harvey B. Simon, M.D., Harvard Medical School.

> New studies show that it's possible to attain nearly all the health benefits of exercise without high-intensity

activity that leaves you drenched in sweat. That means moderate exercise, such as walking, biking, and gardening can help you get fit. Exercise intensity is less important than the overall amount of time spent exercising, and intermittent exercise is as effective as continuous activity. In fact, golf is beneficial, as long as players walk the course and play two to three times a week.

Research involving more than 320,000 people from around the world proves that regular, moderate exercise can reduce risk factors, such as high cholesterol, high blood sugar, high blood pressure, and high body fat, will improve health, reduce the risk for many chronic diseases, and increase life expectancy.

Moderate exercise is the key to exercising for health. Many will get other benefits by adding exercises for strength, flexibility, and balance, not necessarily in a gym under the watchful eye of a trainer, but at home in a few minutes a day.

A prudent diet is an essential part of a healthy lifestyle to prevent chronic illnesses that plague modern societies.

It has taken the collective effort of many dedicated scientists to bring us back to the of Hippocrates. Some 2,400 years ago, the father of medicine said, "If we could give every individual the right amount of nourishment and exercise, not too little and not too much, we would have found the safest way to health."

(The excerpts above were quoted with the author's permission.)

Summary of the Results	Activity	Benefits
10,269 Harvard Alumni ages 35–74	Walking at least 9 miles weekly	22% lower death rate
	Climbing at least 55 flights of stairs a week	33% lower death rate
73,743 American females ages 50–79	Walking at least 2.5 hours weekly	30% lower risk of cardiovascular events
44,452 American male health professionals	Walking at least 30 minutes daily	18% lower risk of coronary artery disease
39,372 American female health professionals	Walking at least 1 hour a week	51% lower risk of coronary artery disease
72,488 American female nurses	Walking a least 3 hours weekly	35% lower risk of heart attack and cardiac death; 34% lower risk of stroke
30,640 Danish men and women ages 20-93	Spending 2-4 hours weekly on light, leisure-time activity	32% lower mortality rate

(This table was presented here with the author's permission.)

Dr. Harvey B. Simon, MD, is an associate professor of medicine at Harvard Medical School and a member of the health sciences technology faculty at Massachusetts Institute of Technology (MIT). He is the founding editor of the *Harvard Men's Health Watch* newsletter and author of six consumer health books, including The Harvard Medical *School Guide to Men's Health* (Simon and Schuster, 2002) and The No Sweat Exercise Plan: Lose Weight, Get Healthy, and Live Longer (McGraw-Hill, 2006). Dr. Simon practices at the Massachusetts General Hospital; he received the London Prize for Excellence in Teaching from Harvard and MIT.

Summary

We've presented an overview of the body,
the miracle machine we live in.
This miracle machine has a finite life span.
We must treasure it, exercise it,
eat the proper food, drink the right water,
but ***never, never, abuse it!***

Chapter 6

Our Mental Health

You Have A Wonderful Mind; Use It!
A Modern Fable

A man runs to God and complains, "You're so unfair! I can't run as fast as a horse. I'm not as strong as an ox or elephant. I can't fly like a bird or swim like a fish. My eyes aren't as sharp as the eagle's, and my hearing and smell can't match that of a dog. I don't have the sharp teeth and claws of a tiger, and all the time you told me that I'm your favorite!"

"Yes, my son, if I gave you all that, you'd be the laziest animal in the world," replied God with a smile. "You'd be like the male lion that sleeps all day and wakes up only to eat and have sex. I gave you the best gift of all. I gave you a powerful mind. If you use it, you make me smile, because with it you can learn about me, and the infinite mysteries surrounding you. If you don't use it, you cannot survive."

Our Powerful Minds

Anything your mind can conceive and believe you can achieve.
—W. Clement Stone, author and businessman

How does this principle work? A common view of people is that we are a body carrying a mind. We're one out of more than seven billion people on earth. We're just nobodies, trying to survive.

Our physical world consists of our five basic senses: vision, touch, hearing, smell, and taste. Based on our senses, our own world is small. We're not aware of most things occurring around us. For example, in an empty room, at least one hundred channels of TV signals, several hundred radio station signals, and one hundred thousand or more cell phone signals float in the air. We can't see or feel them unless we have some means to receive them. There are also literally millions of germs and bacteria float about us unseen. We can't see electricity, and yet we know that the body functions by electrical impulses. We cannot see gravity, but as we grow older and eat junk food, we feel this force growing stronger.

You are your mind. Minds are not brain cells. To illustrate this metaphor, consider the computer hardware and software analogy. Your brain cells are just hardware. Your mind is programmed by your parents, teachers, God, and yourself. In fact, programming our minds is the common denominator to success or failure.

We have a conscious and subconscious mind. These two minds create the person within, the true us. We're not just flesh and bones. We're, in fact, an unlimited mind, housed in a limited body.

The Story of Doug Blevins

Doug Blevins - NFL Kicking Coach (Source: LA Times 2/6/2005)

A picture is better than ten thousand words. To the left is a photograph of Doug Blevins (in wheelchair), who has worked as a successful professional football kicking and punting coach. His coaching career began when the New York Jets hired him in 1994.

Blevins was born with cerebral palsy and yet became one of the most sought-after kicking coaches in the NFL. He cannot walk. His hands are curled so he can't hold a football.

He coached two of the best kickers: Adam Vinatieri of the New England Patriots, upper left photo, and David Akers of the Eagles, lower left. Both kickers were in the Super Bowl in 2005. No matter which team won, Blevins won, and he cannot even clap!

He was later hired as kicking coach with the Miami Dolphins. He guided kicker Olindo Mare to twenty-eight field goals and 117 total points, which was the most points scored by a Dolphins rookie or first-year player. Overall in his career with the Dolphins, Blevins coached Mare to connect for 79.4 percent of field goal attempts, which stands as the highest percentage in club history.

"He sees things the other guys don't see," said Pete Carroll, New York Jets coach, who first hired Blevins in 1994 and later became the famous football coach of (USC) and now the NFL Seattle Sea Hawks. (NFL Super Bowl Champions).

Even with great faith, hope, and tremendous desire, Blevins did not receive new legs or new hands from God. Instead, God gave him a great mind with sound ideas and a burning desire to succeed. He took action and achieved his impossible dream.

Understanding Your Conscious Mind

Your conscious mind is a constant battleground between positive and negative ideas.

POSITIVE	NEGATIVE
Faith	Fear (ill health, poverty, etc.)
Hope	Worry
Love	Greed,
Dream	Jealousy
Ideas and thoughts	Hatred
Desire,	Lust
Knowledge	Doubt
Wisdom, integrity, character	

All these values cannot be seen, but they determine the direction of our lives. Success begins in our minds!

> ***It's not your aptitude, but your attitude***
> that determines your altitude.
> —Zig Ziglar, author and motivational speaker

Dr. Norman V. Peale's top-selling book, The Power of Positive Thinking, taught us how to favor the positive side and develop our Positive Mental Attitude (PMA).

Dr. Schuller's book, Possibility Thinking, takes it one step further and is based on the Bible verse: "With God, all things are possible!" (Matthew 19:26). He taught us how to make our plans with faith in God and take PMA into action to fulfill our God-given dreams.

Understanding Your Subconscious Mind

Our basic instincts, the automatic functions of our bodies, our habits, and our consciences, are programmed and stored in the subconscious mind. It records our emotional experiences: battle scars, sins (dark secrets), etc. Our habits, good or bad, are formed here.

The Power of the Subconscious

A two-thousand-pound elephant was killed in a circus fire while chained to a small stick hammered to the ground. The question is why the powerful elephant didn't free itself since it could easily pull the stick out of the ground. When the elephant was young, it had been tied to the same kind of chain tied to a tree. It tugged and tugged, but couldn't free itself. Soon, that behavior and result were burned into the elephant's subconscious so that freeing itself from the chain was impossible, and the animal gave up.

We've all heard stories about a strong war horse that would defend its fallen master against lions and tigers yet would obey the much weaker master's every command. Why? It's the power of the subconscious. In fact, the taming of all animals is through conditioning the animal's subconscious mind. When we were growing up, we heard seven to ten noes to every yes. Sometimes, we as parents meant it for good, but unwittingly programmed our children for failure and develop a *can't*-do attitude instead of a can-do attitude.

Here's an interesting example from ancient China:

> 錢
>
> The Chinese character for MONEY is made of three parts. Each part is a Chinese character in itself. The character on the left means GOLD, which is obvious. The other two are SPEARS. Why two spears? It is believed that the first spear is held by one's conscious mind to hunt for opportunities. The second spear is held by one's subconscious mind (inner self). For most people, the second spear is pointed backward, constantly reminding you, "I don't have the education." Jab! "I can't sell." Jab! When you fail and your spouse says, "I told you so," your subconscious fear is reinforced. This spear goes in the stomach and goes around and around! (Hara-kiri - a form of suicide in Japan).
>
> If you want success, turn the second spear to point outward. With both spears pointing forward, gold will come in!
>
> Your biggest enemy is yourself!

Be an Unconscious Competent

If we want to succeed in anything, we have to learn to be unconsciously competent.

There are three phases of learning. First, we're consciously incompetent, meaning that we know that we do not know but are willing to learn. Second, we learn to be consciously competent. We learn but haven't mastered it. Third, we master it and become unconsciously competent. Now we enter the area of the subconscious in action.

A simple example is our own experience of learning to drive a car. At first, we're consciously incompetent. We've a hard time keeping the car within our lanes and keeping our hands and right foot coordinated to maintain speed. After a while, we become consciously competent and get a license. At this stage, driving is far from being a pleasure. We drive with two hands on the wheel, consciously trying to keep the car safely on the road. We watch the speedometer to maintain speed. It's a stressful experience.

However, as we continue to drive, we become unconsciously competent. Most of the motion becomes automatic, like breathing, and we no longer think about it. The routine role of driving has been relinquished to the subconscious mind. Now driving is a pleasure.

Another example is learning a foreign language. When I came to the States in 1950, I hardly spoke English. My English–Chinese dictionary was my bible. Every time I read my textbook, I had to translate it into Chinese so I could understand it in Chinese. When I tried to speak English, I first think in Chinese and then translated the words into English. I hesitated and stuttered. I was consciously incompetent with English. After a while, I found many technical words were not in my dictionary. I was forced to learn and think in English. I soon became consciously competent. After more hard work, I learned to think and speak in English and slowly became unconsciously competent with dedication and hard work.

Similarly, we learned to play the piano and perform martial arts the same way. We practice and practice until we become unconsciously competent.

An experienced soldier will tell you that in a combat situation, the difference between life and death is often measured in milliseconds. You go through numerous drills until you're trained to react quickly because, in combat, you never have time to think before you act. If you want to be unconsciously competent, learn to use the power of your subconscious mind.

We are the product of our minds.

If you can dream it, you can do it!
—Dr. Robert H. Schuller, televangelist

Every worthwhile thing must be built twice,
first in your mind and then take action.
—Stephen Covey, author

By virtue of the thoughts which they choose and encourage, that mind is the master-weaver, both of the inner garment of character and the outer garment of circumstance, and that, as they may have hitherto woven in ignorance and pain, they may now weave in enlightenment and happiness.
—James Allen, author

The Bigger Brain Hypothesis

Many people believe some achieve greater success because they have bigger brains.

To test that theory, upon his death, Albert Einstein left his brain for research to find out why he was more intelligent than the average. Here are some findings: Einstein's brain was average size and weight. A certain part of his brain was more developed. It's speculated it could have developed due to repeated usage, the way an athlete's muscles develop with repeated exercises.

In elementary school, the slower students may have been teased as "bird brains." Modern research shows that the birds have the highest brain-to-body weight ratio (1/12) compared to humans (1/40). Note that the ratio for the elephant is (1/560); however, because of the elephant's enormous weight, its brain is bigger than ours. There goes the theory between brain size and intelligence.

I submit that many of the great world thinkers may have had a brain (mind) that allowed it to be fine-tuned to the spiritual (invisible) world. Perhaps this happened through the subconscious mind, which seems to transcend time and space. (See Chapter 5.)

I personally believe that many geniuses receive their inspirations from the spiritual world and bring them into reality. Einstein was always inspired to think outside the box; Beethoven was inspired to compose beautiful music he himself couldn't physically hear.

As we examine our minds, the old proverb, "As a man thinks in his heart, so is he," is proven true in every aspect of our lives. Indeed, we are literally what we think. Our character, actions, habits, and accomplishments are the products our thoughts, the creation of our minds.

Modern research has proven that negative thinking, worry, and fear isn't only affecting what we do, but also have a drastic impact on our health. If we want success, the first thing we must do is to develop, control, and expand the conscious and subconscious mind.

The Mastermind Principle

Human minds are powerful. The only thing more powerful is the joining of multiple minds.

When multiple minds are joined for a common purpose, the power rises exponentially. Proof: Henry Ford failed until he met Edison. They both had no formal education, but they helped and encouraged each other to achieve their dreams.

Declaration of Independence (July 4, 1776)

The greatest United States decision was made on July 4, 1776, when fifty-six people signed the Declaration of Independence. They knew full well they would create a free nation or die trying.

What most people don't realize is that the Declaration of Independence was the product of the mastermind of fifty-six people. Their collective thoughts had set in motion what built this nation six years before we won our freedom. They didn't just sign the paper, but each took action in his own way. Success takes sacrifice and commitment.

When you're willing to die for your dreams, nothing can stand in its way.

If you have a dream that you're willing to die for, you cannot fail!

My Own Experience

Here's my own first-hand experience with the mastermind principle. When I entered MIT as a freshman, I knew that to continue my education, I would need scholarships. To ensure my scholarship, I needed to be in the first dean's list, which meant a grade average of 4.5 or higher out of 5.0, which in turn meant at least four A's and one C. Four of the five courses were in science where I felt confident, but the courses in English and the humanities were real problems.

Having never taken a formal course in English, and having learned most of my English from GIs in the aircraft mechanic's school, I was unprepared. When I was given a paperback book assignment in my humanities class, I was supposed to read it in two hours. After two hours, I had read exactly five pages and found over fifty new words. Getting even a C would be a difficult if not an impossible task. ** I sat at my desk, dumbfounded.

Then a schoolmate entered the room and said, "Bob, how do you do this calculus problem?"

I quickly showed him how to do it.

Noticing my predicament, he asked why I was sad, and I told him my problem. He laughed and said, "I read that book in high school. I can help you. If you help me in understanding the science subjects, I'll help you in English."

We formed a mastermind group. Our ground rules were that we would help each other understand the lessons, but we would never cheat by copying from each other.

Throughout my life, this principle has worked beautifully.

** One of my lifelong regrets is that I've never taken a formal course in English. As a result, I always have trouble with spelling and grammar. That's why my daughter was an English major at the Stanford University. Now I have four females—my wife, daughter, and two granddaughters—to correct my English. What a mastermind group! What a blessing!

Two Hungry Men

Two men were starving in the forest because of the severe drought, which had destroyed the crops. They prayed for help. Soon an old fisherman came, carrying a basket full of fish and a fishing pole. He told them they could each have one, either the fish or the fishing pole.

One of them was so hungry that he quickly decided to take the fish and went his way to prepare his long-awaited meal. The other took the fishing pole and headed for the ocean, thinking about all the fish that he would catch with it.

Unfortunately, the one with the pole passed out before reaching the ocean and starved to death. The one with the fish later starved to death also when he finished the basket of fish.

When they checked into heaven, the Lord asked why they arrived before their time. After hearing their sad tale, the Lord said to them, "All you had to do was to form a team and share the fish until you reached the ocean. I had an ocean full of fish waiting for both of you."

Build the Rainbow of Your Success

Helpmate or Dream Killer

One of the most common complaints of entrepreneurs is that their spouses do not support them. In fact, they're often their biggest critics and dream killers.

Based on the Chinese philosophy of yin and yang, woman and man are opposites.

Since caveman days, men have been hunters and providers, and women have taken care of feeding the family. Men want adventure; women want security. Women are satisfied with a rabbit a day so long as the family eats. Men want the bigger and bigger game.

Sometimes the hunter may become the hunted. So what?

So before you embark on your big dreams, share it with your spouse. If you can get your spouse to support your dream, you've a leg up over most people. When the yin and yang work together, the whole is bigger than the sum of the parts.

An old American adage says, "Behind every successful man is a strong, supportive woman." (Or a very surprised mother-in-law! – a joke). As one examines the lives of many outstanding men, the support of strong helpmates was indispensable.

Do you know that both Henry Ford and Alexander Graham Bell owed their initial success to their wives? Yes, their wives were their first mastermind partners. When Henry Ford was trying to build his Model T, he needed a foundry to build his engine blocks. The foundry rejected him because he had no credit. He was ready to give up until his wife said, "We have money. You can use the money we saved for the house as collateral. Go build your dream!"

Alexander Graham Bell was ready to surrender his idea of inventing the telephone. He wanted to get a job so he could afford to get married. His fiancée said to him, in no uncertain terms, "If you give up, I won't marry you." Their women wouldn't let them give up. They made history together.

> If you can find a truly good wife,
> she is worth more than precious gems.
> —Proverb 31:10, the Living Bible

Here are two contemporary Christian women who are outstanding helpmates:

Ruth Stafford Peale, wife of Dr. Norman Vincent Peale. Before Dr. Peale became famous, his book, The Power of Positive Thinking, was constant and routinely rejected by publishers.

One day after another rejection, Dr. Peale was so upset, he threw the original manuscript into the trash can and ordered Ruth not to take it out. Ruth obeyed, but she took the manuscript, still inside the trash can, to the next publisher, and the book became one of the world's best sellers!

First published in 1952, the book stayed on the New York Times bestseller list for 186 consecutive weeks. The book has sold more than twenty million copies and has been translated into forty-one languages.

Dr. Peale wrote many more books and was awarded the Presidential Medal of Freedom by President Ronald Reagan. Although Ruth Stafford Peale worked closely with her husband in all aspects of his ministry, she established a separate identity as a religious leader, public speaker, and author.

She was the cofounder, publisher, and chairman of the board of Guideposts. She's a member of the board of directors of the American Bible Society, Interchurch Center, Blanton-Peale Institute, and Laymen's National Bible Committee.

Mrs. Peale has written numerous articles appearing in *Reader's Digest, Woman's Day*, and The Saturday Evening Post. She's the author of Secrets of Staying in Love (1984), published by Thomas Nelson, and A Lifetime of Positive Thinking (2001), and published by Guideposts.

Dr. Arvella Schuller, the wife of Dr. Robert H. Schuller, the founding pastor of the Crystal Cathedral. She not only supported her husband, but also inspired him to greatness behind the scenes.

Here's an interesting story about one of her contributions to the early development of their church, Garden Grove Community Church (now called the Crystal Cathedral).

Many years after its beginning in the drive-in theater, a ten-acre parcel was available for purchase for only $65,000 with $19,000 down and $400 per month for fifteen years. Dr. Schuller believed the location was ideal and invested $1,000 of the church's money to open a 120-day escrow.

Unfortunately, four hours before the close of the escrow, even after he cashed in his life insurance, Dr. Schuller was still $3,000 short. He called Arvella and said, "Honey, it doesn't look like we're going to make it."

"Call Mr. Gray," was her answer.

"But I can't," Dr. Schuller argued. Two weeks earlier, Warren Gray had been sent home from the hospital with incurable cancer.

"Bob, I know that God wants that property. I know you should call Mr. Gray," Arvella insisted.

Thus encouraged, Dr. Schuller called Warren Gray. Mr. Gray was happy to make up the difference before closing time. This was another of God's miracles that worked through people united together with faith.

Note: Warren Gray was a rancher in Orange County. They attended the drive-in church since its first day and never missed a service. His wife, Rosie, had suffered a stroke years earlier and was totally paralyzed. She couldn't walk or talk, but her mind was good. She wanted to go to church, and the drive-in church was Heaven-sent. They were like two angels sent to help build the church. The Crystal Cathedral still has a drive-in feature in honor of Rosie Gray. (See details in Dr. Schuller's book, "Move Ahead with Possibility Thinking.")

Besides supporting Dr. Schuller in building the church, Arvella has been referred to as the "architect of the Hour of Power." She serves as the executive producer and program director for the Hour of Power, which broadcasts in over 174 countries. Under her guidance, she has creatively blended traditional worship with advance technology. She's credited with the early development of the twenty-four-hour New Hope Counseling Center, the Crystal Cathedral preschool, and the ministry's literacy center. She's an excellent public speaker and the author of the book, The Positive Family, published by Doubleday.

Charm can be deceptive and ***beauty doesn't last,*** but a woman who fears and reverences the Lord shall be greatly praised.
Praise her for the many fine things she does.
These good deeds of hers shall bring her honor and recognition from even the leaders of nations.
—Proverb 31:30, 31 (The Living Bible)

Does a good helpmate have to be a woman? No! Sometimes the table is turned. Here's a remarkable story about my good and much-admired friends, Vern and Lavon Dragt.

After Dr. Schuller secured the ten-acre site for the future church in the sixties, he breathed a sigh of relief. However, there was still a $400 monthly payment to be made. Dr. Schuller needed another miracle. That's where Vern and Lavon helped. They were new church members and unknown to them, their weekly tithe of one hundred dollars covered the entire monthly payment.

Vern was a construction worker, strong and athletic, and the breadwinner for a family of a young wife and three young children. One day Vern came home with a headache and found he had polio and had to be confined to an iron lung.

Lavon had to choose either to go on welfare or go to work. Lavon chose to find work— no easy task for a mother with three small children. She had no experience, no special skills, and no college degree. She found an ad that reads, No experience necessary. "That's for me," she said.

She applied, and the job turned out to be an opportunity to sell Tupperware. "All I have to do is talk, and I have lots of experience doing that," she said.

She became very successful in building her business.

In the meantime, Vern recovered, but his arm muscles had deteriorated, and he could no longer do construction work. He returned to school to get business training and took over the "back office" of his wife's thriving business. They developed one of the single largest sales organizations of the Tupperware Company, and Lavon became its international vice president.

They're constantly increased giving (tithe) to the church helped not only to pay off the mortgage on the church property, but also helped build the Chapel in the Sky at the top of the Tower of Hope.

They also contributed to build the large basketball courts under the Family Life Center of the church, where hundreds of neighborhood youths can find a good Christian environment for sports activities. Having the privilege to serve on the church board with them and attend many Bible studies in their home, I know firsthand that they are a humble couple and perhaps don't even want their story told.

However, in the spirit of the poet Henry Wadsworth Longfellow, I feel that their story will inspire many who are going through life's tough challenges.

> Lives of great men all remind us,
> We can make our lives sublime,
> And, departing, leave behind us
> Footprints on the sands of time;
>
> Footprints, that perhaps another,
> *Sailing o'er life's solemn main,*
> A forlorn and shipwrecked brother,
> Seeing, shall take heart again.

> Let us, then, be up and doing,
> With a heart for any fate;
> Still achieving, still pursuing,
> Learn to labor and to wait.

> —Henry Wadsworth Longfellow
> (Quotes from A Psalm of Life)

The moral of these stories is the importance of teamwork or a mastermind alliance. We have a world of treasures waiting for us if we have a good team and work together.

For Christians, there's an important Bible promise regarding the mastermind group.

> Where two or three of you have gathered
> together in my name,
> there am I in the midst.
> —Matthew 18:20

If you're looking for inspiration and guidance, you'll have the Master himself in your mastermind team. What more can you ask?

> It's important to build
> a mastermind team.
> Where dreams are shared,
> actions are encouraged,
> ideas are nurtured and brought into fruition.

> Find someone to share your dreams,
> share your knowledge,
> encourage and support each other.

TAKE ACTION DAILY!

Chapter 7

Creativity and Applied Wisdom

> There is a Solution to Every
> Problem; Think outside the Box.

In my freshman year at MIT in 1951, one orientation speaker gave this profound remark: "In science, everything that moves obeys just six basic laws: Newton's three laws of motion, the law of gravitation, and the first and second law of thermodynamics. Most of you know these laws. If you don't, you can memorize them in thirty minutes. We keep you here for four or more years to help you develop your mind and learn to think."

Indeed, all creative solutions in science and engineering, as well as the world's problems, came from "thinking outside the box." The reason this important principle has been presented last is to emphasize that "thinking outside the box" can be dangerous if it's not constrained by the other principles and values. For example, one can easily think of new ways to break the law, cheat, and hurt people for personal gain.

Little Johnny's Prayer

Ten-year-old Johnny's good friend got a new bike for his birthday. So Johnny wanted a new bike too for the summer. He'd been a naughty boy. He skipped school often, did not do his homework, and often hung with the wrong kids. His parents told him to straighten out, be good, and pray to God. Maybe God would give him the new bike.

Johnny started his campaign. His first prayer, "Dear God, I'm a good boy. Please give me a new bike." Nothing happened. Then he realized that it was a lie.

So he started again. "Dear God, I've been bad, but not as bad as others. Please give me a new bike." Nothing happened. He started again. "Dear God, if you give me a new bike, I'll be a good boy." Still nothing happened. He was frustrated.

One day he went with his parents to church and spotted a small statue of the Virgin Mary. When no one was looking, he stole it and hid it under his bed. Then he prayed again, "Dear God, I've got your mother. If you want her back, give me a new bike."

Clearly, this is a joke. It does, however, illustrate the danger of thinking outside the box without the guidance of wisdom and a good sense of values.

The Egotistical Woodpecker

One of the woodpecker's main purposes in the circle of life is to keep the trees healthy by removing (and consuming) the insects and worms from the bark and inside the tree.

This one is working very hard building its own image and in the process is destroying the tree, as well as its own source of food!

It may seem humorous, but just think about the leaders in history who destroyed much of the world trying to build their own self-glorifying legacies.

Indeed, not knowing your God-given purpose and mission in life can lead to destructive behaviors.

This picture was found in The New Yorker on Jan 23, 2012. (Reprinted here by permission)

>Learning without thinking leads to confusion.
>Thinking without learning is dangerous!
>—Confucius

>Learning with thinking leads to WISDOM.

From the book of Proverbs in the holy Bible to the writings of numerous ancient Chinese scholars, wisdom's virtue and value are universally regarded as important. The Chinese word for wisdom is Zhi Hui (智慧) and consists of two characters. The first character means intelligence, and the second character is added to imply "beneficial intelligence" or understanding.

We can infer from this that there's a difference between wisdom and intelligence.

Intelligence alone, without the guidance of wisdom, can cause great harm. Hitler, Rasputin, and many hardened criminals are typical examples. They may have been extremely intelligent, but they lacked the guidance of wisdom. Millions died in World War II as a result of a few men's ambitions to rule the world.

Wisdom implies the ability to use one's intelligence and education to make choices, following principles that benefit others as well as one's self. That's why we must conduct our lives well and guide our lives with wisdom.

Boxed-in Thinking

From infancy to adulthood, we're taught to do tasks a certain way. We follow the instructions and don't ask why. This is what I call "boxed-in thinking."

Example 1: The wife a newlywed couple asked her husband to help her saw off the two ends of the ham before she baked it. He asked why. She said her mom makes the best ham, and that's the way she did it. Soon her mother came to visit. When asked the same question, her answer was, "My mom always did it that way, and she made the best ham."

Grandma came to visit. She laughed as she answered the question. "We had a small kitchen, and that was the only way I could fit the ham into my tiny oven."

Example 2: Modern science tells us that the best way to grow bacteria and microbes is in a place that's warm and damp - the kitchen dishrag. Yet it's still standard equipment in most households. Imagine a cough or sneeze near the rag from a person with a cold. The germs will incubate and multiply on the rag and soon spread over the kitchen while the housewife wipes the kitchen clean. In the old days, we didn't know better, and we had no substitute for it. Today we have disposable paper towels with wet strength; the dishrags should be retired.

Think Outside the Box

In this modern age of reason and science, it's important to learn to solve our problems by thinking outside the box. When faced with a new problem, don't rush in and solve it the traditional way. Analyze the cause. Think and look for other possibilities.

There is a remarkable US company named Hewlett Packard Company (HP), whose corporate culture (core belief) is "invent". (Read "Built to Last", *Ref.7 Appendix D* for the full description). It's interesting the company chose the word "invent", which is a verb, meaning it's a thinking process, not a goal, which is "invention."

HP actually started with a failed bowling foul-line indicator and a failed automatic urinal flusher. They had good ideas, but they were way ahead of their times. The vacuum tube technology in 1938 was not good enough to be practical. By hanging on, they eventually got their break when the Disney Company awarded them a contract for eight audio oscilloscopes for the film Fantasia.

It's interesting to note how the principles discussed in this book played out in these two companies. The Disney Company used the principle in Chapter 3, following their vision to produce Fantasia, which unknowingly helped HP through the principle in Chapter 1 to get it started. HP, in turn, by constantly applying the principle in Chapter 7 "thinking outside the box," has greatly benefited the world.

Here are examples showing individuals who practiced this principle.

Dr. Robert H. Schuller

In 1955, Dr. Schuller came to Orange County, California, to start a new church. He had $500, a wife, two babies, and an old car with a small organ in tow. He couldn't find any schools or public facilities available for him to start a church the traditional way, so he used the top of a snack bar in a drive-in theater as his pulpit and the theater as his church. His catchy slogan was "Come as you are in your family car." He rang thousands of doorbells and built his church one member at a time. Many clergy criticized him at the time for starting a church at the "passion pit." Thirty years later, that humble beginning became the world-famous Crystal Cathedral. (More details about Dr. Schuller's success can be found in chapters 1 and 2.)

James Hillier and the Electron Microscope

One of the greatest inventions of the twentieth century was the electron microscope. Light microscopes can magnify objects up to two-thousand-fold, whereas the electron microscope can boost it up to a million-fold, making it possible to observe individual molecules.

James Hillier didn't invent the electron microscope; he perfected it and received the prestigious Lasker Award for it. He is mentioned here because of his novel approach to marketing this wonderful device.

After he perfected the electron microscope, he took his design to the Radio Corporation of America (RCA), where he joined the research staff. Because RCA's marketing people were focused on radios and television, Hillier's device was neglected.

As his instrument was a high-ticket item costing more than $10,000 each, no small sum in the sixties, he took it upon himself to do direct marketing to potential customers. He invited fifteen to twenty people from a given discipline who were ideal users of his product, he demonstrated his device, and showed them the benefits. For those with interest, he invited them back for additional training and prepared a user's manual for the customer's specific discipline.

Within two years, he sold more than fifty instruments to fifty pioneers in many different fields. Orders then came in through referrals and by reputation.

Michael Te-Pei Chang

Michael Te-Pei Chang is a former professional tennis player from the United States. He's best remembered for becoming the youngest male winner of a Grand Slam singles title. He won the French Open in 1989 at age seventeen and became the first American man to win the French Open since 1955. He was a hero for both the United States and the Chinese nationals.

Of particular interest is his epic five-set encounter with Ivan Lendl in the fourth round of the French Open, where he displayed his uncanny ability to think outside the box.

In the fourth round of that tournament, he faced the world's number one ranked player and three-time champion, Ivan Lendl. Conventional wisdom made the tall, muscular, and experienced Lendl the heavy favorite to win the match against the fifteenth-seeded, seventeen-year-old, five-feet-seven Chang. This game had the makings of a modern David and Goliath match.

The match appeared to be going Lendl's way when he comfortably took the first two sets 6–4 and 6–4 and then broke Chang's serve in the opening game of the third set.

Chang played on to claim the third set 6–3. Partway through the fourth set, Chang experienced a severe attack of leg cramps. This match was billed as Chang's speed against Lendl's power. With no more speed, Chang resorted to novel tactics by thinking outside the box.

He began by taking speed out of the match by playing "moon balls." He ate bananas, drank at every opportunity, and left the court for an extended bathroom break.

Lendl, who was known as one of the calmest players, lost his rhythm.

Chang further shocked him by delivering an underarm serve and won the point. Lendl was so surprised that he couldn't get to it.

Chang later explained, "I was trying to break his concentration. I would do anything to stay out there."

Barely able to stand and throbbing with pain after many of his shots, Chang continued to battle. Despite being on the verge of physical exhaustion, he fought his way to a 5–3 lead in the fifth set with two match points on Lendl's serve.

Aiming to break Lendl's concentration one more time, Chang stood well inside the baseline, almost at the T-line in the center of the court while awaiting Lendl's serve (normally an almost suicidal position when facing an opponent's powerful serve). This move forced the exhausted Lendl to ace him and produced a double fault, giving Chang the victory, 4–6, 4–6, 6–3, 6–3, and 6–3 in four hours and thirty-seven minutes.

Everyone admired Chang for his courage and cunning after the match. It was a miracle finish! Being a fine Christian, Michael gave the glory to God.

Seven days later, Chang became the youngest male champion in French Open history.

The Second Biggest Piece of Meat

While I was in junior high in China, I was sent to a distant school and stayed in its dormitory. Lunch was our biggest meal. We eat standing around a round table, eight students at a table. We were given a large bowl of steamed rice, and in the middle of the table was a large platter of vegetables with exactly eight pieces of fat meat on top.

Before we ate, we had to sing the national anthem and listen to speeches. While this went on, we students eyed the biggest piece of meat on the platter. When the start signal was given, seven pairs of chopsticks raced toward the biggest piece of meat, while I casually picked up the second biggest piece without any competition.

By the way, no one ever got the biggest piece because it was always mutilated beyond recognition.

Learning this lesson early has helped me always to look and think before I act. Look for alternate solutions and better ways of doing activities. This has led to many innovative ideas and inventions in my later life.

Useful Tips for Applying to Top Universities

Top schools such as MIT, Stanford accepts less than 10% of their applicants (All of them are top students in high school).

Because I was a graduate of MIT and my daughter went to Stanford University. Many parents asked for my advice about getting their children admitted to top schools.

I do not claim to be an authority on the subject matter; however, here are some tips that may help:

Good grades and SAT scores are a must! However, everyone who applies also has that. You must make yourself stand out. How? Here are some tips:

- Leadership qualities – All top schools are looking for future leaders, so show them that you are one. Join some good school activities. (Eg. FBLA, Scouts, book clubs, student governments, etc.)
- Learn social skills. Run for some offices in your junior or senior years. Note: Presidents. Secretaries are very time consuming, try for VP, social chairman etc. it still counts.
- Use music and sports only as recreational activities, unless that is your chosen career path. You must conserve your time. (Don't be neither fish nor fowl!)
- Get good recommendation letters from alumni of the school. Your parents may be able to help from their contacts. Now, you can also search for them among social media profiles and ask them for their advice. If they like you, they will help you.
- When writing your essay for the application, say less about "I, I, I" but more about how you want to make a contribution to the world, these schools have reputations for building people! Include a good smiling picture of yourself. (Check your grammar)
- Clean up your social media, they may check it.
- Dress professionally during an interview. Be the future leader they are looking for.

Finally, do not despair if first you do not get in, go to a lesser school, do well and transfer later. It is much easier to transfer in during the junior year or in graduate school. (Reason: The dropout rate for the top schools is very high, sometimes up to 50%, they may want to replace some of the dropouts with Junior-transfers, if you are ready for it.)

Useful Tips: Handling "tough courses" in college.

While I was an engineering professor at the university, one of my courses is "Engineering Mechanics"- the first core course in engineering. I have over 350 students in the class. It is a tough course and has one of the highest dropout rates! Why? Because for many students, it is the first course that teaches the basic principles in engineering and the students must learn to use them to solve real life problems – one must learn to think creatively.

Many students, who dropped out, blame me for their failures. One of the worst ones was: "Why doesn't he speak English". They don't bother me because "Losers" always blame some others for their failures – my mission is to inspire the winners who really wanted to learn.

Here is a tip that I shared with all the students who came to me for advice.

Divide and conquer!

1. Take a piece of paper. Draw a line through the middle like this:

Things I've learned	Questions

2. Now the enemy has a face! All you need to do is finding the answers to the question one at a time from the teacher,

your study group (mastermind group) or some friends who had already gone through the course.

3. Do not do only the assigned problems from the textbook; do all the others as well.

Why? It gives you more practice. Furthermore, many of your examination problems may come from the un-assigned ones and you are already well prepared! (The only drawback is that some of your classmates may hate you for raising the "Class Average").

So, remember this: "Inch by inch, anything is a cinch! Yard by yard, it is hard". So learn to divide and conquer your questions one at a time!

Useful Tips on Job Search

During my tenure as a professor at UC Irvine, many students asked my advice about finding jobs. They wanted me to look over their résumés to see if they were good enough. Many good Asian students had poorly written résumés. I sent them to my secretary or to an English major to correct their work and then return to me.

I shocked them by saying that good résumés do not get jobs! It gets you in the door, but it doesn't necessarily get you the job. A bad résumé won't get you in the door. So a good résumé is important.

"However, to acquire the job, you must do some additional research; you must learn to think outside the box!" I told them.

"What do you mean?" they asked.

Note that you are in a race against many others with similar qualifications. You must learn to stand out like a "crane among the chickens" (鹤立鸡群 hè l jī qn in Chinese).

Do your research and differentiate yourself.

Here are the reasons:

1. Know your own strength and goal. What are you good at? What kind of job do you want?
2. Research the companies that offer what you want. With the Internet, you can find almost anything about any company: its hot products, its management team, etc.
3. Once you know the information on the company that offers the interview, ask the interviewers specific questions about the company. Get them to do the talking. With your research, you can carry out an intelligent discussion.

Four ways to make a good lasting impression:

1. If you are looking for a professional job, dress professionally. They are looking for the future executives of their company, so look like one.

2. In the meantime, clean up your social media profile. It will be checked. (For Example, if you want to work for the defense industry and you have aired anti-government or anti-war sentiments, you may not get your security clearance!)

3. Print a business card for yourself with your professional picture in it. Why? It makes them take notice. You spent thousands to get an education; a few dollars invested here will be well-spent! It will make you stand out. By the way, when you give them your card, it gives you a chance to ask them for their card. Ask them questions such as: what school did they come from, how they got their job; what advice can they give you, etc.

4. Follow-up later via email and thank them for their time and tips. On your follow-up, always include your professional picture. Another chance to refresh their memory and make a good impression.

> Know yourself, know your adversaries,
> one hundred battles, no defeat!
> —The Art Of War by **Sūn Zi**, (孙子)

Here is my personal experience. During my first job interview in 1956, after getting my master's degree at MIT.

Because I was a naturalized citizen, my background as a teenager in China cannot be checked, and I could not get a security clearance. I was not qualified to work for the prime contractors and the air force. I had to find a job with subcontractors.

During my interview with the head of the research department at the Honeywell- Aeronautical Division, we talked about "frequency response". I casually mentioned the wonders of the human ear. Unknown to me, it was his prime research interest. He had written many papers on the subject. We held an hour-long discussion, with him doing most of the talking and I listened with great interest and asked many questions. The result: I got the best offer in my entire class. Unbelievable!

Later, I learned the reason. Even though a few of my American classmates were better than I was (especially in English), they were going after the prime contractors: Lockheed, North American, Boeing Aircraft Company, etc., where they competed with a multitude of talents. In other words, they were cranes among cranes. They were lucky to get the job. Fewer cranes were where I was. I stood out, and they really wanted me.

Warning: If you want to find a good responsible job, clean up your Facebook and social media profiles and posts. Believe me, they will be checked! This will be a consideration for your promotion too. Many people think that their private life is nobody's business, if so, why post it!

Remember again, a chicken with stretched neck and borrowed feathers is not a crane, so be honest. Here's why!

An Unusual Job Interview

Joe Smith was interviewing for a very important job as a vice president in a bank. He passed all the preliminary interviews. He was one of the few finalists. He was told that the final interview would be conducted by the bank president himself. He prepared extra hard for this as it was a big step in his career.

Upon arrival, the bank president greeted him warmly, grabbed his hand, and said: "Joe Smith, I and my family were looking forward to meet you again! When you save my boy's life from the auto accident, we wanted to repay you for your help but you disappeared before we had a chance to talk to you. All we knew was J. Smith. You were our hero!"

"Sorry," said Joe, "you are mistaken. I never saved anyone in an auto accident." "Are you sure?" said the bank president. "I remember that birthmark on your face, it must have been you! I am so looking forward to have our hero working for us; you can even name your own salary."

"I love to be that person, and I'd love to get the job, but sorry, I am not that Joe Smith. So sorry." said Joe.

At that point, the bank president again shook his hand and welcomed him as the newest member of his bank.

"You see, we are looking for a young man with honesty and unshakable integrity. I do not even have a boy!" said the president.

>Here are some more interesting stories about thinking outside the box.

Selling Combs to the Monks: A Modern Chinese Story

I learned this story in China in 2004. A wooden comb factory was looking for a new sales manager. As the large number of candidates was narrowed to three, and they were given a final test. They were to sell the combs to the temple monks assigned to them and report back in one week.

When they returned, the first one said he had sold one. "This is an extremely difficult task as the monks have no hair," he said. "They laughed at me for trying. Finally, I found one with a head-skin disease and told him that it's not sanitary to scratch his head with his fingers and to use a comb. So I sold one."

The second one reported he had sold ten. "There were ten worshiping stations in the temple," he said. "As it's always windy in these stations, I told them it's not respectful to worship with uncombed hair, so I sold one to each station."

The third person reported that he had sold five hundred and had an order for five hundred more.

"Wow! How did you do that?" the boss asked.

"I asked the head monk what was the average offering from each worshiper. He said around five yen. I told him that I could help him raise the average to ten yen if he would do the following: Announce that anyone who gives ten yen would receive a special comb blessed and marked by the temple seal so he or she could literally comb their troubles away.

Almost every worshiper took the offer. Furthermore, many also gave additional offerings to get combs for their relatives.

"As the comb costs only one yen, spending one to get five is a good deal, so the head monk ordered five hundred more. We can expect a steady order every week."

> Monks do not buy combs for their hair,
> but they buy the benefits!

Below are more Chinese stories, showing wise people in ancient times practiced thinking outside the box.

Creativity and Applied Wisdom

The Slowest Horse Race

Background: Genghis Khan (1167–1227) started as a small tribal chief when he was only thirteen. He became the founder of a vast empire by uniting all the Mongolian tribes. He was one of the greatest conquerors in history. His empire extended throughout Mongolia and China, including parts of Russia, Europe, and the Middle East. He was a powerful warrior, especially skilled in archery. He united the tribes, not only by force, but also through his superior wisdom and political skill. His real name was Temujin. Genghis Khan was a title bestowed upon him later as the "Supreme Commander." This story happened when he was only twelve years old.

The early Mongolians were nomads, like ranchers who lived in tents and moved from place to place in search of water and pasture for their animals. They relied heavily on their horses. In fact, riding horseback was such a part of their way of life that children learned to ride almost as soon as they could walk. As a result, the Mongolians were exceptionally skilled equestrians. Their main entertainment was their weekly horse races within each tribe as well as the monthly horse races against other tribes.

One early morning, twelve-year-old Temujin approached his father, the tribal chieftain. "The geese are flying south again," Temujin said. "My friends and I are going hunting."

"Be sure to come back to the midday race. I have a surprise for you," the chieftain told him.

Getting tired of the weekly race, where the same horses won, the chieftain did something new. He ordered that in the next race, the winner would be the slowest horse, not the fastest. All the tribe's people, who had been getting bored, shouted with joy at the new, unexpected idea.

Quickly every rider mounted his horse. The rest of the people gathered eagerly to see the outcome. At the chieftain's signal, a great horn blew, and the race began.

Soon everyone realized this was a big mistake. Most horses didn't move. Some slowly inched forward, while others actually backed up!

After a couple hours of watching this boring event, the chieftain was sorry he'd given such an order. Unfortunately, in those days, the chieftain's word was law and couldn't be changed. It had to be carried out.

Exasperated, the chieftain summoned all his advisors. "Quick! Find a way to get us out of this. This race is more boring than the old ones. Worse, it's never going to end!" bellowed the chieftain.

"Yes, Great One, we'll do our best," replied the advisors, who looked at each other, desperate for a solution.

Then Temujin returned with three huge geese from his hunting trip. He looked at the sorry spectacle and immediately knew what was wrong.

"I can help you, Father," he said.

"Ha! The little boy has a solution."

The advisors sneered and looked disdainfully at the young boy. "Where did you grow so wise? Playing with the geese?"

Temujin just smiled. "I'll give you my three geese if I can't do it," he bargained with a gleam in his eye. "But you all owe me three geese if I can do it."

The adults happily agreed, including the chieftain. "Stop!" shouted Temujin.

The weary riders looked up.

"The chieftain's race will continue with a new rule. Riders dismount," the teenager ordered.

Gladly, the riders obeyed.

Temujin continued, "Mount your neighbor's horse, and let the race begin again at the chieftain's signal."

The crowd roared with approval, and the riders eagerly clambered on their opponents' horses. The signal was given, the horn sounded, and the dust flew as each rider drove his opponent's horse hard to the finish line, hoping to make his own horse finish last.

All the people applauded Temujin for his clever solution. He smiled and basked in their approval.

The chieftain smiled and proudly patted his son's shoulder. "And where shall we bring all these geese, my son?" he asked.

"To a feast, Father, a feast for the whole tribe to enjoy and celebrate our first slowest horse race," said the boy.

Happily, everyone prepared for the feast. From that day, Temujin gained the respect and admiration of the entire tribe, even his father's advisors.

The Goose Gamble

One year later, Temujin's father died, leaving Temujin to become the tribal chieftain at thirteen years old. Until this time, the people were loyal only to their own tribe. They had no strong sense of national unity. Temujin sensed great strength could be gained in bringing tribes together and decided to unite his tribe with the neighboring tribes. Here's how he accomplished that unity with a one tribe.

The tall, neighboring tribal chieftain, famous for his unsurpassed skill in archery, looked doubtfully at the young Temujin and his team of advisors. He'd heard that Temujin was clever, but doubted what advantage he could gain from joining forces with one so young.

"So you want to join forces, young one," said the chieftain. "You've heard, no doubt, that I enjoy a bit of archery. Let's wager." The neighboring chieftain drew close to Temujin's face, his eyes gleaming. "I can hit a bull's-eye at three hundred paces. If you can beat me at archery, I'll serve you. If I beat you, you shall serve me!"

The sound of migrating geese echoed in the air as Temujin steadily returned the neighboring chieftain's gaze. "Very well," Temujin announced, though his advisors shuddered. He pointed to the sky at the geese flying above them. "I'll shoot down one of those geese, while on horseback at full gallop."

The neighboring chieftain laughed scornfully in disbelief. "Let's see you try, little one. I shall enjoy having you serve me."

Quickly, Temujin leaped to his horse and galloped furiously across the plain. Carefully, he took aim and with one swift move, shot down a low-flying goose.

Thunderous applause rang out among both tribes.

The neighboring chieftain's jaw dropped, and he quickly knelt in allegiance to the young boy with the incredible skill.

Words of Temujin's skill and wisdom spread across the land, and people began to write songs about this remarkable feat. As his reputation spread, Temujin was soon able to unite all the Mongolian tribes began a great nation.

Comment: Actually, Temujin's "goose gamble" was not such an amazing feat. Modern physics teaches that it's much easier to shoot a low-flying goose at full gallop than to do so while standing still. At a full gallop, if the speed of the horse matches that of the goose flying in the same direction, Temujin was shooting at a target as if it were standing still. (The principle is the same as that in the movies where the cowboy chases the train and easily jumps over when he catches up with it.)

However, to be able to discover that principle at such a young age, before much was known about modern science or physics, was truly amazing.

The Stinky Swamp

Background: This story happened during the Tang Dynasty (500 AD) in the capital city of Cheng-An. In ancient China, there was no social security as we know it. When people grew old, the business was always passed on to the eldest son. The household power and duties then passed to the eldest son's wife. In this way, the old folks were well taken care of by the younger people. Sometimes this system didn't work perfectly.

Build the Rainbow of Your Success

* * *

Mr. Chang lay dying on his bed. He summoned his two sons to give them final instructions. He gave his oldest, a forty-five-year-old son, the business, the house, and two-thirds of his money and land holdings. To his fifteen-year-old son, Bao Bao (meaning treasure), he gave one-third of his money and one-third of the land holdings.

"This is unfair," the wife of the oldest son said. "You labor day and night for your father's business for twenty years, and Bao Bao only eats and goes to school. He never helps with the work."

"Woman, we have plenty. After all, he's my brother," oldest son told her. "All right, you can give him the money, but I will divide the land," said the wife.

"Okay, okay. Don't bother me anymore," the oldest brother said as he walked away.

Among the father's land holding was a stinky swamp. Near the center of the capital, the land was a worthless, dead pond where all of the city's rainwater accumulated. In the summer, it stank. The government officials had served the family notices that they should fill it or pay a heavy fine.

"I know. We'll give the stinky swamp to Bao Bao. It's a hot potato out of our hands," the wife said. "It's like killing two birds with one stone." With this decision, she instructed Bao Bao to move from the house to his own land, knowing very well that Bao Bao would have to spend all his money just to fill the pond. He would have nothing left to build a house or start a business. It serves him right for stealing my husband's father's affection all these years, thought the wife.

Having no place to stay, Bao Bao was taken in by a poor uncle, who lived near the swamp. He owned a small Xiao Ben (Chinese pancake) shop. His entire family lived upstairs and was barely getting by.

One day, Bao Bao got a great idea. He bought several red flags and tied each on top of long poles. He put the poles inside the swamp. He told all the children that anyone who could hit the flagpole with a stone could get a red ticket, which they could redeem for a fat pancake in his uncle's store.

Soon all the kids in the city joined in the contest. When they exhausted all the nearby stones, they took bags to gather stones outside the city. Many wealthy parents sent their servants with carts to supply the stones for their kids. It was a big event! Even the royal princes wanted to try their skills.

In the meantime, the uncle's shop prospered. As the winners redeemed their tickets for fat pancakes, all the other kids and their parents purchased one, too. There was always a line out the door.

As the pond was being filled with stones, Bao Bao kept moving the flagged poles toward the center.

Three months later, the swamp was filled and ready to be divided into housing lots. Since the land was located in a choice location near the center of the capital, rich men bought parcels for their homes and made Bao Bao a wealthy man.

Furthermore, the governor noticed Bao Bao's wisdom and made him an official. His uncle also became successful and was able to open a big restaurant.

When the world gives you lemons, make lemonade!

***There's a solution to every problem, if
you learn to think outside the box!***

Chapter 8

White – The Ultimate Solution

As you've read this far, you know there are seven aspects of your life that need your constant attention. It's easy to understand but hard to do.

You need a good friend to mentor, guide, and encourage you constantly along the way. In this world, we have many friends. However, how many are truly good friends who really know us? Here's a famous Chinese quote (of the same words):

péng	**yǒu**	**mǎn**	**tiān**	**xià**	**zhī**	**jǐ**	**yǒu**	**jǐ**	**rén**
朋	友	滿	天	下	知	己	有	幾	人

Indeed, how many of your friends truly know and care about you? When you're lost, how many will show you the way? When you are hurting and discouraged, how many will comfort you? When you're sick or in trouble, who will give you hope and strength to move on? Is there such a friend who sticks closer than a brother?

Yes, I've found such a friend! Let me introduce you to Him.

His name is Jesus Christ, the Son of God!

What? Did I shock you?

He is my personal best friend. He can be yours, too. If I'm preaching to the choir, great! If not, let me share with you God's plan for you and me.

I was an atheist for a long time. I found that most religions represent people's efforts to reach for God or to try to be good enough for Him. I later found that Christians believed just the opposite. Christians believe God came to reach people and to make it so that we wouldn't have to be good enough for him. He sent Jesus in human form as a bridge to reach us. God prepared and planned for us to have a close relationship with him. Christ's goodness and sacrifice on our behalf made that relationship possible. All we have to do is to accept the gift by faith!

> For God so loved the world,
> that he gave his only begotten Son,
> that whosoever believes in Him should not perish,
> but have everlasting life.

God did not send His Son into the world to condemn the world, but that the world through Him might be saved.
—John 3:16, 17

> If you confess with thy mouth, "Jesus is Lord,"
> and believe in your heart
> that God raised Him from the dead, you will be saved.
> —Romans 10:9

Once we accept Christ as our personal savior, here is His promise:

> If you abide in my word, you're my disciples indeed.
> And you shall know the truth,
> and the truth will make you free.
> —John 8:31, 32

> Abide in me, and I in you,
> as the branch cannot bear fruit of itself,
> unless it abides in the vine,
> neither can you unless you abide in me.
> —John 15:4

What? He abides and dwells within me, just by accepting him? How can that be?

The reason that you ask this question is because you can read and understand this passage. How? Your knowledge and wisdom abide and dwell within you, though you can't see them. It is with your spirit, also.

Does this mean you are given instant sainthood if you accept Christ? No. You've started your spiritual kindergarten and learn to love your new found friend and perfect mentor, who can help you throughout your life.

The recurring theme of this book is that we live in two worlds: the physical world we can see and touch, and the invisible spiritual world. We have a physical body and a spiritual body. In our spiritual body, wisdom, knowledge, character, integrity, spirit, and soul dwells. When we add God to our spiritual world, it goes to infinity!

> For the things which are seen are temporal, but the things that are not seen are eternal.
> —2 Corinthians 4:18

It's the most important thing for us to add Christ to complete our life in this world and the next. He is like the white **light that contains all the rainbow's colors and can** easily help us strengthen any color of our own rainbow.

Many people refuse to believe in the existence of God. I, myself, began my life as an atheist. I believed science had or will have all the answers. I believed all religions were crutches for the weak and superstitious.

However, as I got more education, I found that the more I knew, the more I knew that I did not know. For example, in astronomy, we believe that the universe began with hydrogen and gravity. The gravity compresses the hydrogen, creates nuclear fusion, a "Big Bang" occurred, and here we are.

Wait a minute. What exactly is gravity and where did the hydrogen come from? We do not know. They just are!

I used to believe "When we die, we're dead. Period, it is the end!" However, deep inside, I knew that we were more than just our physical body. I had seen people die in hospitals. All their organs were still in the body, but the life was gone! Where did it go? I had no answer. I realized that other than my stubborn pride, I had no answer. I was trying to play God by pulling myself up by my bootstraps.

In trying to find the truth, a friend suggested I look within and write a book about my own life.

First chapter: The past. Has it been good? Did I do anything I regretted? Did I hurt people? Do I need forgiveness? In short, am I perfect thus far?

Second chapter: The future. Where am I going? What do I want to do? Do I want to be famous and rich? Do I want to make a contribution to the world? What, where, and why?

Last chapter: Did I have a good rainbow? Did I live? Did I make a contribution? When my physical life is over, will I be six feet underground with a tombstone marking my entrance and exit to life? Or am I going to be free to enjoy an eternal life in my spirit with God?

After much contemplation, I realized that in physical life, we eat, drink, work, raise a family, grow old, and die. In spiritual life, we're concerned with...

1. What is truth?

2. What makes things right or wrong?

3. What is our purpose and mission in life?

4. Where do I go when physical life ends?

In searching for the answers, I found them in the Bible. (See my own story later in chapter 9). I found that: Christ is the visible expression of the invisible God. He is the only one in history that came back from death to show us the truth.

Once you've accepted Christ as your personal savior and friend, he'll abide in you, to help you find your purpose, determine your mission, and pursue it with a passion. His spirit lives within you to give guidance daily onto eternity.

As a rocket or space scientist, let me share a metaphor. We're like a spaceship, built for a "special purpose" by our maker. To be useful, however, we need a mission. We need someone to set a destination, plot the course, put in a propulsion system to get us moving, and give us a guidance and control system to keep us on course. At the end of the journey, when all the power is exhausted, hopefully we'll have reached our destination. Without the intelligence, power, and guidance behind us, we're a useless hunk of metal; full of potential but with nowhere to go.

That's why I believe in a personal God with whom I can communicate and from whom I can receive guidance and strength. Many people think having a personal God is like putting ourselves into a straitjacket. There are too many rules and too many "Don'ts."

On the contrary, I found that there are a lot of things we should do. Once God gives us a purpose, mission, and vision, He gives us the power to fulfill them. We experience true freedom. We'll receive corrections (Don'ts) only when we've drifted off course.

How can you prove God exists? If He does exist, how do you know He will have anything to do with us?

For your first question, without the clock, can you prove time exists? Similarly, with gravity, we can't see it, but we know time and gravity have profound effects on our lives. Before I came to America, it was just an area on the map.

I finally proved that it existed when my plane landed in California. So, if you want to experience God, take your spiritual journey.

To answer your second question, I ask you to "come and see" and look at the "footprints on the sand."

In the last two thousand plus years, our personal God has been working among us. Look at the hospitals, schools, universities, and humanitarian organizations that have been built to honor His name and testify to His profound influences.

Shortly after our independence, 106 of the first 108 colleges were started in the Christian faith. By the close of 1860, there were 246 colleges in America; seventeen of these were state institutions, other than that, almost everyone was founded by Christian denominations or by individuals who avowed a religious purpose. Harvard, Yale, Princeton, Dartmouth, Brown, Columbia, University of Pennsylvania, and William and Mary are typical examples and the list goes on and on. (Just Google it to find the details)

Below is a beautiful, short essay about Jesus.

One Solitary Life

He was born in an obscure village. He worked in a carpenter shop until he was thirty. He then became an itinerant preacher. He never held an office. He never had a family or owned a house. He didn't go to college. He had no credentials but himself. He was only thirty-three when the public turned against him. His friends ran away. He was turned over to his enemies and went through the mockery of a trial. He was nailed to a cross between two thieves. While he was dying, his executioners gambled for his clothing, the only property he had on earth. He was laid in a borrowed grave.

Nineteen centuries have come and gone, and today He is the central figure of the human race. All the armies that ever marched, all the navies that ever sailed, all the parliaments that ever sat, and all the kings who ever reigned have not affected the life of man on this earth as much as that one solitary life. —Dr. James A. Francis (1928)

On Evolution

"Wait a minute!" you may say. "As a scientist, don't you believe in evolution?" Yes, I believe evolution is an excellent study of the orderly creation process. Furthermore, I believe the creative process continues. God is working on the development of our minds now.

I've personally seen the evolution of digital computers. First, I saw the Whirlwind computer, developed in 1950 at MIT, which contained thousands of vacuum tubes and relays that occupied an entire floor. Then I saw the development of transistors, computer chips, and now microchips. If I didn't see the intelligence behind it, I could easily conclude that microcomputers evolved from the huge Whirlwind computer because the basic operating principles remained the same.

Similarly, if humans suddenly disappeared, another being may conclude that all buildings evolved from mud huts to houses to buildings and to skyscrapers because of the basic structural principle, "the triangular frame," is maintained throughout all. Yet, who started the mud huts?

On Science

Some of my scientific peers told me that accepting God and His teaching by faith is not intellectually honest or satisfying. Where is the proof?

I shared with them my experience in physics. As every scientist knows, this simple formula, $E = MC2$, by Dr. Albert Einstein is the treasured truth on the altar of science. However, less than 0.001 percent of the humans ever experimented with it. Most scientists and engineers accepted it by faith. More than 95 percent of the educated people don't even know what it means. These people may be well educated in other areas, but they are ignorant in atomic physics. Just because most people do not know it does not mean it is less true.

When I was taught this formula in MIT undergraduate physics in the fifties, the professor said: "This equation shows that the energy within just one kilogram (about two pounds) of matter can light a 100-watt light bulb for several hundred million years! So don't worry about the sun burning out soon."

I asked my professor: "Why does 'energy' have to do with the speed of light squared? Why not $E=1/2 MC2$ like that of kinetic energy ($1/2 MV2$) in Newtonian mechanics? Have you actually experimented with it?" His answer was: "Do you believe in the atomic bomb? In science, all physical laws are derived by someone through inductive and deductive reasoning. You have to accept what you are taught by faith and build on it." My professor then added: "If you want to prove everything we are going to teach you yourself before you accept it, you will be here forever!"

I asked him another question: "Since this is an equation, I can divide both sides by C2. We get: $E/ C2 = M$, is this equation reversible?" Can energy be transformed back to mass?

"I honestly don't know," said the professor. He then added jokingly, "If you find out, let me know!"

Dr. Einstein worked very hard on his unified field theory trying to find the answer. It remained elusive in his lifetime.

However, just recently in 2012, the "Higg's boson," also known as the God particle, was discovered and has shed some light on this matter. It appears that this newly discovered particle is extremely unstable, has no spin, and cannot be seen except in a high-energy collision in the Hadron Collider. However, it is called the God's particle because it is believed that the "Higg's boson" gives all other atomic particles their mass. Incredible!

Finally, is this the evidence of energy converting to mass? Interesting!

Have we found the final solution now? No, we may have just taken another step toward deeper science! A case in point: photons and infrared radiations gave us light and heat. They have no mass! Why? Imagine a photon of light coming to our eyes at the speed of light, if it has any mass at all, its momentum MC will destroy us!

Is my belief in the existence of a personal God still irrational? At this point, I will not debate with you further. I've done my share of debating in college. I firmly believe now that debating is like arguing with one's spouse. One never wins; it just damages the relationship.

Instead, "come and see." Let me invite you to a party and introduce Him and some of His friends through the ages to you. If you are skeptical, but not stubborn, take a good look at the people listed below.

Here's a partial list of famous scientists in history whose intellectual capacities were superior to most, and all of them have made significant contributions to the development of modern science. They were also strong believers in God.

We begin and end with two of the most well-known men of science: Isaac Newton and Albert Einstein.

Sir Isaac Newton (1642–1727)

Newton was famous for his work in optics, mechanics, and mathematics. Newton was a figure of undisputed genius and innovation. In his system of physics, God is essential to the nature and absoluteness of space. In the Principia, he stated, "The most beautiful system of the sun, planets, and comets could only proceed from the counsel and dominion of an intelligent and powerful being." Newton was also a well-known, part-time preacher.

Nicholas Copernicus (1473–1543)

Copernicus was the Polish astronomer who put forward the first mathematically based system of planets circling the sun.

Sir Francis Bacon (1561–1627)

Bacon was an English philosopher known for establishing the scientific method of inquiry, based on experimentation and inductive reasoning.

Johannes Kepler (1571–1630)

Kepler was a brilliant German mathematician and astronomer. He did early work on light and established the laws of planetary motion about the sun. Kepler was an extremely pious Lutheran.

Galileo Galilei (1564–1642)

The Italian Galileo is often remembered as a Christian who also ran into conflict with the Roman Catholic Church when his controversial work on the solar system was published in 1633. Because he believed the earth revolved around the sun, he was put on trial. After the trial, he was forbidden to teach the sun-centered system he'd discovered.

Rene Descartes (1596–1650)

Descartes was a French mathematician, scientist, and philosopher who was called the father of modern philosophy. He had a deeply religious faith as a Roman Catholic. God was central to his whole philosophy. Rene Descartes and Sir Francis Bacon (1561–1626) are generally regarded as the key figures in the development of scientific methodology.

Blaise Pascal (1623–1662)

Pascal was a French mathematician, physicist, inventor, writer, and theologian. He was raised a Roman Catholic, but in 1654, he had a religious vision of God, which turned the direction of his study of science to theology.

Thomas Bayes (1701–1761)

He was an English mathematician and Presbyterian minister, known for having formulated the Bayes's theorem, a mathematical theorem for calculating conditional probabilities. (Part of my doctoral thesis was "The Bayesian Approach to Statistical Estimation.")

Robert Boyle (1791–1867)

One of the founders and early key members of the Royal Society, Boyle gave his name to Boyle's Law for gases and wrote an important work on chemistry. As a devout Protestant, Boyle took a special interest in promoting the Christian religion abroad.

Michael Faraday (1791–1867)

Michael Faraday FRS, the son of a blacksmith, became one of the greatest scientists of the nineteenth century. His work on electricity and magnetism not only revolutionized physics, but also led to many inventions that influence our lifestyles today. Including things like electrolysis, computers, telephone lines, and websites. Faraday was a devout Christian.

Gregor Mendel (1822–1884)

Gregor Mendel was the first to lay the mathematical foundations of genetics in what came to be called Mendelianism. He began his research in 1856 (three years before Darwin published his Origin of Species). He was a Catholic friar in Austria.

Louis Pasteur (1822–1895)

He was a French chemist and microbiologist. His discoveries reduced mortality from puerperal fever, and he created the first vaccines for rabies and anthrax. His experiments supported the germ theory of disease. He's regarded as one of the main founders of microbiology.

William Thomson (1824–1907)

Scotsman William Thomson was foremost among the small group of British scientists who helped lay the foundations of modern physics. He was also a committed Christian.

Max Planck (1858–1947)

Planck made many contributions to physics, but he is best known for quantum theory, which revolutionized our understanding of the atomic and subatomic worlds. Planck was a German church warden from 1920 until his death and believed in an almighty, all- knowing, beneficent God.

Albert Einstein (1879–1955)

Einstein is probably the best-known and most highly revered scientist of the twentieth century and is associated with major revolutions in our thinking about time, gravity, and the conversion of matter to energy ($E=mc2$). He had a firm belief in God. Among his quotes were:

"I want to know His thoughts, the rest are details."
"Science without religion is lame,
religion without science is blind."
—Albert Einstein

Recently, another famous scientist, Dr. Francis Collins (MD and PhD) turned from atheism to Christianity. He is the current director of the National Institutes of Health (NIH). He served as director of the National Human Genome Research Institute at the NIH from 1993 to 2008. He was awarded the Presidential Medal of Freedom in November 2007 and received the National Medal of Science in 2009. He recently wrote a book, "The Language of God," which documented his experience from an atheist to a Christian after studying the complexity and the wonders of the human genes.

Finally, I want you to read the words of one of my heroes, a fellow rocket engineer and scientist and founder of Astronautics, Dr. Wernher Von Braun, (1912 to 1977). He was responsible for the design and realization of the V-2 rocket for Germany during World War II. After the war, Von Braun worked on the U.S. Army's Intermediate Range Ballistic Missile (IRBM) program. Following the launch of the Soviet Union's Sputnik 1 on October 4, 1957, the U.S. Army Ballistic Missile Agency was directed to launch a satellite using its Jupiter C rocket trying to catch up. This program was developed under Dr. Wernher Von Braun's direction. It was successfully launched on Jan31, 1958.

Dr. Von Braun later joined the National Aeronautics and Space Administration (NASA) as director of the Marshall Space Flight Center. He was the chief architect of the Saturn V launch vehicle, which propelled the Apollo spacecraft to the moon. According to one NASA sources, he is "without doubt, the greatest rocket scientist in history." In 1975 he received the National Medal of Science.

Here are his direct quotes:

"The two most powerful forces shaping our civilization today are science and religion. Through science, man strives to learn more of the mysteries of creation. Through religion, he seeks to know the creator. Neither operates independently. It is as difficult for me to understand a scientist who does not acknowledge the presence of a superior rationality behind the existence of the universe as it is to comprehend a theologian who would deny the advances of science."

"Far from being independent or opposing forces, science and religion are sisters. Both seek a better world. While science seeks control over the forces of nature around us, religion controls the forces of nature within us." (Dr. Wernher Von Braun, 1963)

There are also more than fifty Nobel Prize winners in science who believe in God, just Google them. There is a website, www.asa3.org, where you can find more information.

In summary, I want to share with you the important reason why all these outstanding people found faith in God. It is not only for the forgiveness of sin, but also for the inner peace with God through Spiritual rebirth. It frees us from anxiety, guilt, depression as well as a negative self- image. The stress flows out as salvation flows in. They knew that physical body ebbs away, our spiritual body continued to grow. When God is in it, it goes to eternity!

Jesus said to Nicodemus (a ruler of the Jews), "Most assuredly, I said to you, unless one is born again, he cannot see the Kingdom of God… That which is born of the flesh is flesh, and that which is born of the spirit is spirit." John 3:3-6

At this point, if you would like to join this group of friends, just accept God's invitation:

Behold, I stand at the door and knock.
If anyone hears my voice and opens the door,
I will come in to him and dine with him and he with me.
—Revelations 3:20

All you have to do is open your heart and invite him in as your personal Savior and friend. Join a Bible-believing church, study the Bible, and grow in your faith.

On the other hand, if you're still skeptical, but not stubborn, take this advice from the Time Magazine's Man of the Century - Albert Einstein.

Condemnation (rejection) without investigation is the height of ignorance.

Please make your own investigation. I suggest you begin with the four gospels in the New Testament of the Bible. Then read the following books:

1. The Purpose-Driven Life by Rick Warren, a number one best-seller that examines the question, "What on Earth am I here for?" (Ref. 19, Appendix D)

2. The Case for Christ (Ref. 23, Appendix D) by Lee Strobel. Lee is a lawyer and journalist. He also was an atheist and a spiritual skeptic. His many books document his search for God and examines the evidence from an investigative lawyer's viewpoint.

3. Mere Christianity (Ref. 22, Appendix D) and many other books by C. S. Lewis, a brilliant Oxford University professor, who made a similar journey. His book, Mere Christianity, remains one of the clearest elucidations of the basic truths of Christianity and has helped many people to find faith.

4. The Language of God (Ref. 20 Appendix D) by Dr. Francis S. Collins, (MD and PhD), Director of the National Human Genome Research Institute (NHGRI) and famous scientist who turned from an atheist to a Christian after studying the wonders of the human gene.

5. Many books by Dr. Robert H. Schuller. (Ref.10, 11, 12 Appendix D).

6. Confidence in the Bible by Harold J Sala (Ref.24 Appendix D).

Chapter 9

Footprints on the Sand

I have always been impressed with the story by Mary Stevenson about a man who dreamed he was walking on the sand with the Lord. He noticed two sets of footprints. One set belongs to him, and the other is the Lord's. He also noticed sometimes there was only one set of footprints during his most difficult times.

"You promised me Lord, that if I followed you, you would walk with me always. But I have noticed that during the most trying periods of my life there have only been one set of footprints in the sand. Why, when I needed you most, you have <u>not </u>been there for me?" he asked.

The Lord replied, "The times when you have seen only one set of footprints, is when I carried you."

I invite you to walk with me as I share my personal life experiences

Why I Believe in Tomorrow

I will look forward to tomorrow. Some may say, "At the age of eighty-four, how many more tomorrows do you have?" My answer is, "I believe in God and eternity. The brightest tomorrow is yet to come."

I believe that our lives are gifts from God, and what we do with our lives are our gifts to God. So long as there is a purpose in our lives, the tomorrows will always be bright.

Our life is a gift!

We did not choose to be born, yet someone gave us life.
We did not know how to talk, but someone taught us to speak.
We did not know how to cook, but someone fed us.
We did not know how to read and write, but someone paid
the tuition, someone built the schools,
someone trained the teachers,
and someone else wrote the books.
Looking back on our lives, from infancy to adulthood,
Someone has been always there helping us in our development.
These people appeared like angels to touch our lives. They
may not have wings, but they helped us soar.
They gave and they gave, yet were often rejected
and unappreciated.

What should we do with our lives then?
Should we be like the Dead Sea and hold on to all the blessings for ourselves? Or should we be like a live, vibrant lake

that lets the blessings flow out to others?
Should we be like angels without wings to administer to people in need as part of the grand plan designed by the Almighty?

Looking at our children and grandchildren, They require a lot of work and care.
But the blessings they give us are beyond compare.
There is a saying that says it is more blessed to give than to receive.
By giving, we are touching the river of lives that are to come. And we cannot help but thank God for a glimpse of eternity!
—Dr. Robert C. K. Lee, author 10/22/2003

My Story

This is my story told in chronological order. Some of them had been told in earlier chapters, they are being repeated here in more detail.

When I was six years old and living in a rural area of China, I contracted pneumonia. In the 1930s, pneumonia in China was like a cancer, almost like a death sentence. People told me that my mother sat up all night holding me while I burned with fever and spat up blood.

I asked my mother, "Will tomorrow come?" She was crying, helpless, and without much hope.

Fortunately, we could borrow a car and drove several hours to a missionary hospital in Guangzhou. There, an American doctor saved my life. Perhaps I was too young and perhaps I was influenced by my peers, but despite receiving such a gracious blessing, I didn't accept Christianity then. I will always remember and be grateful to the doctor, who had come thousands of miles to give me "tomorrow."

When I was about twelve, we ran as refugees from the invading Japanese army. During a bombing raid, my mother and I hid under a black umbrella by the riverbank. The enemy biplanes flew so low that I could see the pilots' white scarves, waving in the wind. As the bombs fell on the bridge, I saw bodies blown up. I kept asking my mother: "Where is our Air Force?" She said we had none. I swore then that when I grew up, I would join the Air Force and shoot down all the enemy planes. In 1945, the war was over and so was my dream of joining the Air Force. My love for airplanes had just begun.

The Communists took over China in 1949, so I was forced to escape to Hong Kong (then under British rule) and leave my native country. I came to the United States in 1950, in my late teens, to study aircraft and engine mechanics. Many people asked if I was afraid to travel to a strange land without relatives or much money and I could not speak much English.

As mentioned in Chapter 2, I can honestly say fear never entered my mind, perhaps because my sense of mission was too strong. Yes, I had a strong mission when I flew to the United States. It had been a big sacrifice for my parents to send me to America. I had to do well and graduate in one year, get my aircraft and engine mechanic's license, and find a job. With the money I earned, my mission was then to bring my three brothers and six sisters here, one by one, to allow them to study and to give them a "bright tomorrow."

My Interesting Experiences in America

An interesting incident happened when I first arrived at the aircraft mechanic's school in California. I hardly spoke English. Most of the students were veterans on the GI Bill. A large group was from Hawaii. Seeing that I was an Asian kid who didn't know much, they "adopted" me. I hung out with them. For the first few months here, I thought that "pidgin English" was correct American grammar.

My First Job

In the second month after I arrived in the States, I learned an important lesson: poverty is a mental condition. I had little money, but I never felt poor. I found a job sweeping the airplane hangar floors for the Lockheed Aircraft Company, every Saturday. I worked for ten hours and earned $1.50 per hour for eight hours, plus two hours overtime at time-and-a-half. The income fed me for a whole week. In this country, no one needs to be poor if one is willing to work. The money will come sooner or later if one has a positive attitude, develops a plan, and acts on it.

The "Magic Dime"

After I got a job sweeping floors on Saturdays, I needed one more job for Sunday evenings. I got a gas station attendant trainee's job at a local station. In 1950, gasoline was only twenty cents a gallon and there were no credit cards. The gas boy pumped the gas, checked the oil, cleaned the windshield, and collected the money and tips. For the first couple of shifts, magic silver dimes mysteriously appeared everywhere around my station, on my water buckets, cleaning rags, etc. Since they were not mine, I returned them to the station owner. After I was hired, the magic dimes disappeared. I did not realize until much later that it was a test for my honesty and integrity. Fortunately, I passed.

A Terrifying Experience

When I first arrived at the school, I had a schoolmate who weighed more than three hundred pounds, a veteran of Middle Eastern descent. He used the words for S.O.B. in full in almost every other sentence. I checked the dictionary. There was no such word. In a seemingly appropriate moment, I used the phrase on him.

He lifted me with one hand and pinned me to the wall. "Did you call my mother a dog?" He fumed.

I remember yelling: "Don't know your mom! Don't know your mom!" Fortunately, my Hawaiian buddies arrived, surrounded him, and rescued me.

I mention this incident to remind all to be gentle with foreigners. Unless one is a Native American Indian, we are all immigrants or descendants of immigrants. Everyone had a hard time learning the English language and trying to assimilate into the culture when they first arrived. Don't laugh at their broken English. Extend a helping hand!

When I came to America in 1950, I was a typical modern Chinese student. I worshipped science and considered all religions superstitions and crutches for the weak. My major problem was that my dormitory didn't serve food on Sundays.

Since I had no means of transportation, I had to walk miles for food.

Then a gracious American lady, Mrs. Grannas, invited me, a stranger, to her home for Sunday dinner with her family. She first picked me up for church, and then we drove to her house for dinner. I did not become a Christian, but I did receive a "certificate of faithful attendance" from the church. I truly appreciated her kindness, and the Sunday dinners were heaven-sent.

Later that year at a Christmas party, she gave me a Bible. I was disappointed. I thought I at least rated a tie! (See footnote at the chapter's end.)

Despite my language problem, I graduated from the aircraft mechanic school in 1951 with honors. I was ready to find a job.

Unfortunately, my family was forced to move back from Hong Kong (then under the British rule) to China and was not allowed to leave it. I became a man without a mission. I decided to enter college.

I asked a teacher about the best engineering school in the United States. He told me Massachusetts Institute of Technology (MIT). Like a typical, optimistic kid, I told him I would attend MIT.

He laughed and said, "Bob, you don't know where it is and you can't even spell Massachusetts." He was right, of course, and I'm not sure I can spell it now. But I could spell MIT!

Even though I didn't believe in God, by a strange change of destiny, I now call a miracle. I was accepted at MIT to study Aeronautics and Astronautics (now called Aerospace Engineering). I was again given a new tomorrow.

I was so excited when I arrived at MIT in 1951, I went to the book store (called the COOP) to buy my foot-long slide-rule. (Needed for all scientific calculations; there was no PC or iPad in those days). I clipped the slide-rule on my belt and felt like the newest gunslinger in town! Then the textbooks weighed heavily on my hand. I wondered how I could understand all that... well, one page at a time.

Throughout my first five years at MIT, I held true to my belief that science had all the answers. Many Christians have tried to influence me, but my ego was strong so none succeeded.

One friend was my fraternity brother, William Wu. Even though I turned a deaf ear to his witness, I did sense a quiet, unique quality about him that I didn't have. Because of his untimely early passing, I was never able to thank him for sharing his faith with me. I still hold his memory in fondest regard.

In the meantime, different people often help me in my needy hours. I was surprised that most cared for me without demanding anything in return.

I am particularly grateful to Mr. C. T. Loo, who provided the C. T. Loo Fellowship for me. (See his story in Chapter 2).

During my senior year at MIT, I was involved in a minor traffic accident. Their lawyer literally took me by the feet and shook every penny out of me. I was totally broke. Without the fellowship, I would have had to drop out of school and work as an illegal immigrant!

Some people would say that I won this fellowship fair and square. Looking back, I'm truly thankful that someone—a total stranger—was willing to give unselfishly to empower a needy young man with a "new tomorrow."

In graduate school, I discovered a shocking truth: the more I learned, the more I knew I didn't know. Each new discovery leads us to a deeper mystery.

Though science has made tremendous strides, we are usually stuck when we ask a series of basic questions such as:

Q: Why is the grass green?

A: Because it contains chlorophyll.

Q: Why chlorophyll?

A: It is needed to convert carbon dioxide into oxygen. It is part of our ecosystem.

Q: Why?

A: It just is.

Before my graduation, someone gave me two challenges:

1. Study the hummingbird, Bob. You know aerodynamics, mechanics, control, and navigation, but can you build a hummingbird? Do you believe that nothing built it? (Yes, I did study it; see the answer in Appendix A.)

2. What is the most powerful thing on Earth? An idea! Look around. Nothing built by people is ever started without first having an idea. Can you weigh it, measure it, see it, or define it? However, ideas exist. Look at all the wonderful things, living or not around the world. Something made them, whether you can see it or not.

After earning my master's degree, I was offered an excellent job in the research division at Honeywell in the aeronautical division in Minneapolis, Minnesota.

For the first time, I had a goodly amount of money. I bought a new car, a new stereo system, a TV, a hunting rifle, a shotgun, and everything else a young bachelor would want all on **credit!**

I did well in my work. Yet, my life felt empty. Some unknown things were missing. I was challenged by these questions: What is truth? What makes something right or wrong? What is the meaning and purpose of my life? Is tomorrow just more food and drink and work? I felt like a person all dressed up with no place to go.

I hunted the answer to four important questions:

1. Is anybody up there?
2. Does anyone care?
3. Why am I here?
4. Where am I going?

My Search for God

As I searched for the answers, I found Sir Isaac Newton was a great scientist and also a fine Christian. He was an excellent, part-time preacher. Some people asked him, "Why, when faced with such a wonderful gospel message, do some people still reject God?"

He answered, "Sometimes I've absent-mindedly tried to light my candle with the extinguishing cover on. It wouldn't work. It is not that the candle doesn't work, but something I did block it from lighting."

Everyone has his own blocker. My ego was mine. With my education and intelligence, I proudly presumed my intellectual ability probably ranked in the top US percentiles, if not in the world. Yet the more I studied the beauty and design of nature, the more my own work shrank to insignificance. Being in awe of the complexity of nature, we're faced with a great dilemma. To say that "nothing" or "time" alone has built the world takes a great deal of faith in "nothing." (The second law of thermal dynamics would also have to be thrown out!)

Many scientists believed we came from the big bang, a cosmic accident. But what caused the big bang? Where did all the hydrogen and gravity come from?

Surprisingly, I was introduced to God through the study of babies.

When I found God in 1956, I was a bachelor. I came across a book that presented pictures of baby's development from month to month prior to birth. Unfortunately, that old book can no longer be found, however, we can get some up to date pictures from Google. Ref: <u>Robin Elise Weiss, LCCE</u>, Pregnancy and Childbirth expert

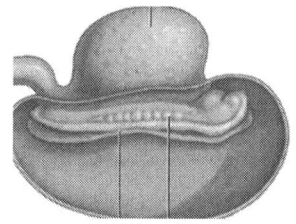
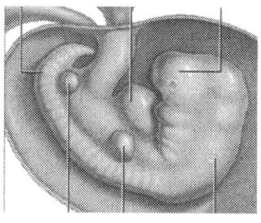
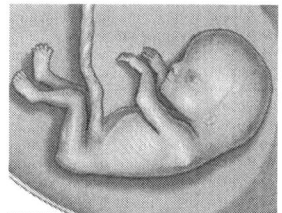

The pictures shown the baby at 5th week; 6th week and 9th week. Note that in the 9th week, the baby is fully formed, it weighs just **one ounce**!

From the study of biology, I knew about sperm and egg cells. Once they unite, they started splitting like all cells.

However, how did some cells become the liver, kidneys, brain, skin, and bones?

Furthermore, how does the baby know the correct areas to place these organs in the body and connect them so they work properly? Do you know that the baby's heart starts beating at the fifth week after conception, and there's no blood yet to pump? We did not know much about genes and DNA in 1956. Today we know much more about them, and yet the mystery deepens. (See The Language of God by Dr. Francis S. Collins. Ref. 20, Appendix D)

As a scientist and aircraft mechanic, I knew how to build an airplane. One must carefully design it, build the parts and fit them together carefully and connect all the wirings. One must test them to make sure that they all work together.

How does a baby know to do that? Some well-meaning Christian friend told me that the Bible says: "We're wonderfully made." And then he quoted me the scripture: "For you (God) created my inmost being; you knit me together in my mother's womb" Psalm 139:13.

Ha! There had to be a good scientific explanation. I started my investigation.

One night, questions hit me like a ton of bricks. Here are the questions and my answers:

1. Did I invent the Chinese and English language? No. Someone taught me.

2. Did I learn to read, write, and speak by myself? No. Someone taught me again.

3. Did I write the textbooks? No. Someone else did.

4. Did I invent and discovered that we came from monkeys all by myself? No. Someone taught me again.

5. If I did find scientific explanations about how babies grow from some papers or books, someone will be teaching me again.

People told me the Bible had the answers. Should I reject that without studying it? Furthermore, Sir Isaac Newton believed in it. And he certainly was no dummy. I also remembered what Einstein said:

"Condemnation (Rejection) without investigation is the highest form of ignorance"

I got off my high horse and opened my mind to investigate by studying the Bible. By chance, I was invited to a Chinese Christian Fellowship meeting by my friend Fred Shaw (Hsiao). CCF was started by an old widow, Mrs. Torjeson. Her husband, a missionary to China, was killed during World War II. Mrs. Torjeson single-handedly and successfully raised four small children while starting this organization. She was a slightly built, poor widow, but had a tower of strength. Largely, through her effort and the love of her organization, I was challenged with questions and found my answers in the Bible.

For example, I found my pride was a sin. Yes, I was like an ignorant, prideful man who refused any spiritual instruction, yet knowing deep down, I did not have the answers.

Someone once said that the Bible is an acronym for:

Basic **I**nformation **B**efore **L**eaving **E**arth. Interesting!

Once I opened my mind and heart, I made my peace with God and started my spiritual journey and adventure. Countless Chinese students from the university also discovered Christianity at the same place. Truly, what Mrs. Torjeson did will echo loudly in eternity!

One question lingered: If there was a God, why did he let bad things happen? Why are there cancers, diseases, and crimes that kill good people?

The Bible gave me the truth. God gave us free will, and we make our own choices and suffer the consequences. For example, the best Christian will be killed if he chose to fire a pistol to his head. Similarly, cancer will happen if he keeps eating the wrong food and drinking the wrong fluid.

God never promised us the sky will always be blue and life will be smooth sailing after we become a Christian. He promises to be with us throughout life's storms if we remain faithful. Furthermore, everything physical in nature dies and has the formula for renewal built in. However, the human soul and spirit, like an idea, have no shape and form, cannot be destroyed, and will continue into eternity with him.

> Life is real! Life is earnest! And the
> grave is not its goal;
> **"Dust thou art, to dust returnest,"**
> was not spoken of the soul.
> A Psalm of Life by Longfellow

When I studied the Bible, I was in awe of the life of Jesus. Despite being born in an obscure town and with no formal education, his teachings, in only three years, changed the world.

The life of Jesus is a miracle. No one in history has ever achieved so much with so little. When one studies the Bible, one is impressed with his life. One is faced with a choice. Either Jesus is the Son of God as he claimed, or he is a madman. His claim leaves no room for in between.

God may choose to save our bodies if he wishes, as evidenced by the stories in the Bible. He performed numerous miraculous healing. However, his main mission was and is to save souls.

The Bible said, "All of us have sinned and come short of the glory of God."

Jesus said, "That which proceeds out of the heart (soul) of man defiles the man." In other words, God examines the heart (soul) and sees if it is pure. If it is not, he will cleanse it.

God's plan of salvation gives our souls a bath by cleaning it with the blood of Christ through faith.

At first, I had problems accepting it because I thought it was too simple. However, after some contemplation, I realized that if God, with his infinite intelligence, Wants to communicate with people, he must address us in the simplest terms, so all People can understand and benefit from it. It is like giving a portable radio to a savage. All he has to do is turn the knob to access the technology behind it. Understanding of electricity and electromagnetic theory are not required.

Likewise, by the simple exercise of faith in Christ, our spirits can be connected to his, and he will live within us! It is incredible, but true.

Some skeptics say, "Prove it."

My answer is, "Come and see, and experience it yourself." God has already revealed himself in the simple terms that we all can understand. All we do is accept the gift. God gives us a free choice. You can take it or reject it.

After I accepted Christ, I shared God's plan of salvation with an engineer friend.

"Are you telling me that God can cleanse our sins with Christ's blood?" He asked. "Don't tell me you believe in that stuff, just good old blood? I thought you were a smart fellow from MIT."

"No," I said. "God used a super highly refined organic polymer with a complex chemical formula, which begins with $C_{738}H_{1166}N_{812}...Fe+$, with an iron core. This substance also contains hemoglobin, amino acids, proteins, and millions of living organisms. Each has a specific cleaning function to perform." (It was a brief description of "good old ordinary blood" in scientific terms.)

"Now that's more intelligent," he said. "Still, who is God anyway?"

I was often asked the question: "Why does God have to save us by using a baby born of a virgin and later die on the cross for us?" My answer is "Why not?" In fact, whatever God chooses to do, the unbeliever will ask "why" again.

With a little knowledge, one can easily be an intellectual skeptic; only **by faith** can one join *God's army* and march into the spiritual world.

After I became a Christian, in 1957 I married my wife, Bettie, a fine Christian woman. We started tithing. We thought life would be smooth sailing from then on. Unfortunately, our big test came three months later.

"Black Thanksgiving" came just before Christmas that same year. The large contract the company had won—the

B-70 super bomber project—was abruptly cancelled. A massive layoff ensued. Every engineer who had worked with the company less than eighteen months was let go.

With only fourteen months of work, I got a pink slip. I thought I did very well in my research, had received a patent, and had excellent results. I could not understand how this happened. It was so unfair! My hope of a promising career was dashed to bits.

A Lesson about "Dancing in the Rain"

After the initial emotion subsided, the wisdom of the Chinese proverb I had learned since childhood returned to me:

sāi   wēng   shī   mǎ   yān   zhī   fēi   fú
塞　　翁　　失　　馬　　焉　　知　　非　　福

Literally, it translates to "Mr. Tsai lost his horse. Who knew it wasn't a blessing?" Here's the brief story:

> A servant went to Mr. Tsai and reported his prized white stallion had run away. All the people said, "It is bad luck you lost your best horse."
>
> "It is not necessarily bad," Mr. Tsai answered.
>
> The next day, the servant reported the white stallion had returned and brought ten wild horses with him. One was a beautiful, golden stallion, a perfect warhorse. All the people said, "Wow! Very good luck."
>
> "It is not necessarily good," Mr. Tsai answered.
>
> Soon Mr. Tsai's son started to train the wild golden stallion and broke his leg. All the people said, "It is bad luck. He is your only son."

"It is not necessarily bad," Mr. Tsai answered again.

A month later, a war broke out, and all the able-bodied young men were drafted and killed in the battles. Mr. Tsai and his lame son enjoyed their old age surrounded by many grandchildren. Read "Wu and the Golden Stallion" *(ref. 30,* Appendix D) for more details.

We also remember the verse in the Bible:

Be anxious for nothing,
but in everything by prayer and supplication,
with thanksgiving, let your request be made known to God.

—Philippians 4:6

We decided to "let go and let God" and committed our problem to God through prayer.

A series of miracles happened that again gave me a "new tomorrow."

A couple of days after my layoff, the chief engineer in engineering asked if I would like to work for him in the advanced development department. He told me that wanted me since my interview with the company, but the research department had first choice.

I jumped at the chance. I was assigned to design the control system for the MISS project, which stands for Man In Space Soonest (a terrible acronym). It was the forerunner of the Mercury Space Project. This eventually led to the company being awarded the Gemini and Apollo projects. I'm not claiming credit for these developments. It took a team of engineers to accomplish that. However, having a chance to be a pioneer in this area was an honor and a real blessing.

After the MISS project, I was put in charge of the flight-test program of the Adaptive Control System, I invented in research, and the company was awarded a US patent for it.

This system was successfully flight-tested on a F94C fighter and eventually helped the company to win a multi-million dollar contract for the X-15 experimental space plane.

Even though I was a naturalized US citizen, I couldn't get security clearance because I had lived in China as a teenager, and my background couldn't be checked. As a result, I couldn't work on important projects for the air force. Fortunately, both Senator Humphrey and a Minnesota congressmen recognized my contribution to the company and introduced special bills on my behalf. I was granted security clearance by an Act of Congress. Wow! What a country! This act would open up another "new tomorrow" for me, to work for the Aerospace Corporation – the think tank for the Air Force a few years later on top-secret space projects.

In 1960, I wanted to return to MIT for my PhD. I was very confident that I would be welcomed back with open arms. However, the timing was not right! God had better plans for me.

In 1961, I applied again. Then unbelievable miracles began. Besides assistantships, I was offered a half-time job by the Raytheon Company near MIT, a strong competitor of Honeywell. The pay was much better than that of the research assistant from the school; furthermore, they would also pay for my tuition, books, and moving expenses too. Wow!

When I tendered my resignation to Honeywell, my boss said: "Over my dead body!" He told me to wait for him to work something out. A week later, I was granted an educational leave from Honeywell at **full salary**. All I had to do was (1) return during vacations and summer to consult with the ongoing projects and (2) work part-time for the Honeywell Boston division on the Optimal Control Project. They also paid for my tuition and moving expenses. Wow!

We couldn't believe this unexpected miracle would last. As soon as we found a place to stay, my wife found a job in the registrar's office at Harvard University. We could live on her salary and banked my entire paycheck - a truly unbelievable blessing.

On November 29, 1963, I was given the most precious Christmas gift. My one and only daughter, Doreen, was born. The timing couldn't have been better. Working on a doctoral program at MIT was extremely demanding. She arrived when my thesis was finished, and we could devote our time to caring for her and enjoying her.

In early 1964, my doctoral thesis, "Optimal Estimation, Identification, and Control," were accepted and surprisingly was selected to be published by the MIT press as the twenty-eighth research monograph. (MIT selects one or two outstanding doctoral dissertations to be published as a research monograph each year.) This was an unexpected honor.

As one drinks water, always think of the source.
—Chinese Proverb

In that spirit, I want to thank Dr. Y. T. Li, my thesis advisor at MIT, for his direction and guidance. A special thank you and acknowledgement is made to Dr. Yu-Chi Ho, Gordon McKay Professor of engineering at Harvard University, a good friend and a wonderful teacher, for his patience in helping me through the threshold of modern control theory.

In the beginning of my book, I also wrote:

Prayer of Thanksgiving

Before God, all men are equally foolish,
for we cannot comprehend all the infinite mysteries
surrounding us.
If there is a grain of wisdom in this work,
may it be to his glory,

For he alone has provided me with this splendid opportunity for learning: Wonderful parents, teachers, and friends, a harmonious home, excellent health, and strength ever sufficient from day to day.
—Dr. Robert C. K. Lee

Many people asked if this prayer was appropriate for a scientific book.

"Why not?" I said. I was truly thankful for all the miracles in my life, and I'm very grateful for them.

Dr. Albert Einstein said, "There are only two ways to live your life. One is as though nothing is a miracle. The other is as though everything is a miracle." I chose the latter.

A year after my graduation, I was offered a dream job at the Aerospace Corporation, the think-tank for the air force. I worked on large rockets such as the Titan II and Titan III space boosters, the Gemini space program, and some top-secret satellite projects.

The titan 3-C Launch Vehicle & Gemini Launch Vehicle

In 1968, I was offered a tenured professorship at the University of California in Irvine (UCI). We moved to Orange County and another "new tomorrow" dawned.

Miracles continued in my life. A notable honor was being selected to serve as an elder in the church that became the Crystal Cathedral. I was privileged to participate in the building decisions of the Crystal Cathedral. I learned first-hand the strength of the founder, Dr. Robert H. Schuller, a great leader and man of faith who overcame many impossible odds.

That's why, when given the opportunity to help translate Dr. Schuller's book: "Move Ahead with Possibility Thinking", into the new Mao script (modern simplified Chinese), I jumped at the chance. The book was published in Hong Kong and has sold several million copies in Hong Kong and China. As this was a nonprofit venture, the profits from the book sales were reinvested in translating many other Christian books into Chinese.

Please do not think I am bragging. I am truly amazed and thankful that God allowed the six-year-old whose life the missionaries saved long ago to begin to bear fruit for His kingdom and to give something back.

As my pastor, Dr. Schuller often said, "Any fool can count the seeds in an apple; only God can count the apples from one seed." Looking back, I can see now that my whole career really began with that "Lay-off" in 1957. So, when you face life's storms, keep your faith, sunshine is coming!

Another miracle happened in 1967 when I could bring my sister and her family to America from China. Her three children were reaching college age during the Chinese Cultural Revolution. If they had stayed in there, they would have no chance for higher education. By coming here, they were able to go to college. Two have become successful engineers, and the third is a well-known physician. I'm not claiming credit for their successes. They achieved those themselves. However, to be able to give them an opportunity for a brighter tomorrow at that precise time was a miracle of God and a blessing for us all.

In the seventies, we invested in a small business in Laguna Beach. The business required a twenty-by-eight-foot, illuminated sign for advertisement. I secured the permit and spent several thousand dollars to have it built and installed. A few years later, Lady Bird Johnson (President Johnson's wife) started the National Beautification Program, which required all cities to remove large signs. We protested because (1) we had the permit for it, (2) we needed the sign for the business, (3) it had cost thousands of dollars to install and would cost us more to remove it, and (4) the city should at least grandfather us in.

The city's answer was no!

I was very upset. My wife suggested we again let go and let God and committed it to prayer. "Are you kidding?" I responded. "How do I pray for an electric sign?" Nevertheless, we prayed about the injustice of it.

Within a week, an Alpha Beta supermarket delivery truck smashed the sign to bits. Their insurance company paid for the cost of the sign and its removal. Furthermore, our business increased because of local publicity!

This was a solution we couldn't have imagined. Why? We had been in that shopping center **more than five years**, and every night delivery trucks drove around the parking lot. One may say that it was a lucky coincidence. I call it an answer to prayer. What do you think?

> Does God answer prayers? Absolutely!
> However, God is not your genie.
> His answer may not always be yes.
> But if it is, be very thankful!

Our most recent miracle is my wife's recovery from Acute Myelogenous Leukemia (AML) in 2006. She was in and out of the City of Hope Hospital for nine months. At her age, the doctors estimated her survival chance to be between 2 to 5 percent.

After the first few weeks of chemotherapy treatments, her blood count dropped very low. When the nurses gave her blood transfusions, her blood count did not rise as expected. When they tried to give her platelets, her body suffered chills and shook violently because it rejected the introduction of this foreign material. With low platelets, she could have easily suffered internal bleeding that will threaten her life. We were helpless but not hopeless! We again let go and let God and enlisted our Christian friends to pray for her.

One night as I slept on the sofa in her hospital room, she screamed. Before I called the nurses, I moved close to her bed. She repeated, "Thank you, Jesus! Hallelujah, Hallelujah," several times and then returned to sleep.

In our forty-nine years of marriage (in 2006), she had never expressed herself that way. I took out her notebook and wrote, "May 10, 2006, 11:24 p.m., GVB (God visited Bettie)."

The next morning she told me she had had a nightmare. She dreamed she was in a dark room where many half-naked midgets were attacking her. Each midget had red marks on his naked chest. She was helpless. She saw she had a red mark, too. She screamed for help! Then she felt a presence, and every one of the red-marked little people left quickly, and her red mark disappeared, too.

After that day her blood count improved, but always tested very weak. She was able to accept the platelets donated by her brother, Gee. At her discharge from the hospital, she was told to return every three months for a blood check as well as a bone marrow biopsy.

"What can I do to keep her cancer from returning?" I asked the doctor. "We'll see," was the reply.

"What will you do if it returns? More chemo?" I asked.

"We'll see," was the reply.

No advice was given as to what she was to do, eat, drink, etc. I was disappointed.

Later, I learned that most doctors will not give advice outside of medicine and hospital procedures because if anything bad happens as a result of that advice, their liability insurance will not cover it.

We prayed that God would show us a solution.

Shortly after that, we found the Kangen Water - ionized, alkaline water produced by a machine made by the Enagic Company in Japan.

My Experience with the Kangen Water

When I was introduced to the Kangen water machine in July, 2007, I was skeptical because I had learned water can be ionized in freshman chemistry at MIT. (In fact, electrolysis of water was discovered by Michael Faraday in the 1800s. See chapter 8). However, we never learned how this water would benefit our health. I have had type 2 diabetes for many years as well as other health issues such as high blood pressure and high cholesterol, etc. I tried the Kangen water.

After only three weeks, here were my test results:

	Before	Three weeks later
Triglycerides	438	113
Cholesterol	220	151
Glucose	154	104
A1c	7.8	6.4

My blood pressure also became normal.

Wow! After more research, I found that there are considerable scientific basis behind this water. I bought the machine knowing that it was not only good for me, but also learned the water might help my wife, Bettie, to recover from her cancer.

After drinking the water for a few months, my wife's immune system was strengthened, and her blood work began to improve. After a year,

her blood tested normal. Praise the Lord! Her doctor was pleasantly surprised. I told her about the water.

"Whatever you're doing, keep on doing it," the doctor replied.

How and Why Alkaline Water Works

Is this miracle water? No. Neither is it medicine!

We live in a miracle machine. Your body is made with about 75 percent water and about five dollars' worth of chemicals. How it works, grows, and maintains its health is still a mystery.

Our bodies, we have discovered, have a built-in system to maintain proper balance so we can survive in a hostile environment. For example, a body has an efficient temperature regulation system. It keeps its inner organs at around 98.6 degrees Fahrenheit, so that they can function properly. This process is one aspect of <u>homeostasis,</u> a dynamic state of stability between our internal and its external environment.

When the body temperature increases significantly above normal, a condition known as hyperthermia occurs. That's why many poor elderly people die when a heat wave hits. (No air-conditioning).

The opposite condition, when body temperature decreases below normal levels, is known as hypothermia. We can help the body in that condition. For example, a simple warm blanket can become a life-saving miracle.

Similarly, we have an efficient system to help us maintain a proper blood glucose level. However, if we eat unhealthy foods, drink the wrong water or too many sodas (which are very acidic with pH as low as 2.4), we'll become obese and eventually overstress the pancreas and become diabetic.

One of our most tightly regulated systems is blood pH. The ideal blood pH is 7.365. It can vary only a small amount and still keep our cells alive. When blood pH is lower than 7.2, cardiovascular complications can occur. Our bodies will do anything at the expense of our bones, organs, and other tissues to keep the pH at the proper level.

Most of us are polluting our bodies with too much acid-producing activities, among them smoking, drinking too much alcohol, and eating excessive amounts of acid-producing foods and drinks, such as dairy products, sugar, animal protein, processed grains, junk food, and soda (pH 2.4 very acidic).

Recent research has found that while we blame the fat from fast-food restaurants for creating obesity, actually the unlimited soda fountain is the real cause. With a pH of 2.4 and loaded with sugar (nine teaspoons of sugar in each twelve-ounce cup), we become overly acidic. Over time, these factors add to produce the toxic liquid called acidosis, which causes our blood regulation system to "rob Peter to pay Paul," taking calcium and other minerals from the body to balance our blood pH. As this continues, our vital organs can begin to shut down, and our bones become brittle. If this acidic state continues, the result is chronic disease, cancer, and even death.

Fortunately, this acidity can be reversed if we catch it in time. Like a simple blanket can save us from hypothermia, if we act in time, eating more alkaline fruits and food, and drinking alkaline water can neutralize this acidity and revitalize our organs and health.

Are you drinking water from your own sewer?

A friend of mine was suffering from severe constipation. I told him that he may have been drinking water from his own sewer! What? He was very indignant at that suggestion. I told him that we were made of 75 percent water. During normal operation of the body, we use up a lot of water—sweat, evaporation, urine, etc. If we do not drink enough water, the body takes the readily available water from within the colon! Once the water is taken out, we are left with dried waste products, which are difficult to pass. I told him to make it a habit to drink eight to ten cups of Kangen Water per day regularly—no more constipation!

Here is an easy test for dehydration. The color of your urine should be pale yellow. If it is tea color or dark brown, you are dehydrated. When that happens, your cells may be drinking water from your own sewer. Yuck!

It was also found also that the Strong Kangen Water pH 11.5 is very effective in removing **pesticides** from our fruits and vegetables to prevent it from hurting our babies. (see details in appendix E)

(For more information on Kangen Water: go to www.vibrant-health-solutions.com take the tour and get a free e-book.)

On Conflicts between Religion and Science

Many people often asked how I resolve the conflict between religion and science.

To me, there is no conflict because one deals with the physical world and the other with the spiritual world. Many great scientists believe in God. (See details in Chapter 8).

Sir Isaac Newton, a lay preacher, said, "I do not know what I may appear to the world, but to myself, I seem to have been only a boy playing on the seashore, and diverting myself in now and then, finding a smoother pebble or a prettier shell than ordinary, whilst the great ocean of truth lay all undiscovered before me."

Below are the three quotes from Dr. Albert Einstein:

- "My religion consists of a humble admiration of the illimitable superior spirit who reveals himself in the slight details we're able to perceive with our frail and feeble minds."

- "Science without religion is lame. Religion without science is blind."
- "I want to know God's thoughts; the rest are details."

Conflicts only occur when so-called experts in one field display their proud arrogance and ignorance of the other. Both sides are guilty of these offenses.

On the religious side, Galileo suffered greatly at the hands of the Catholic Church, because he believed Earth revolved around the sun. The clergy of his time said, "Geometry is of the devil. Mathematicians should be banished as the authors of all heresies."

In 1633, Galileo was tried before the Roman Inquisition and forced to "curse and detest" his own work. His accusers actually believed they were serving God.

Another saying from some of the clergy was pronounced when the Wright brothers were testing their flying machine: "If God wants men to fly, we'll have wings."

I encountered religious zealots before I became a believer. It had to do with the "star of Bethlehem" in the Christmas story. They insisted an actual star shone on the city itself. I told them that's nonsense!

First of all, where did this star came from? What galaxy? What magnitude? Indeed, if a star came that close to Earth, the gravitational pull and the heat would cause us to explode. Furthermore, the light from the star couldn't be focused into a beam (that was pre-laser days) and shine only on Bethlehem like a spotlight. This kind of scientific ignorance had a negative effect on me and stopped me from looking at Christianity for at least two years.

Surprisingly, after I became a Christian, I encountered this question again. I explained it this way. Suppose God said to the three kings, "I'll send a helicopter ahead. You follow its searchlight." No problem! Do you think God, maker of the universe, could make a searchlight without a helicopter?" Imagine our ancestors saw and recorded this event more than two thousand years ago. They saw a guiding light. It was not the sun. It was not the moon, and therefore, it must have been a star. There's no error in the Bible, just our interpretation of it.

Did God really do that? I don't know, but it is very plausible.

One need not use a butcher's ax for an ox to kill a chicken.
—A Chinese Proverb

I do not believe God, with his infinite intelligence, needs to go through all the trouble of moving a physical star from some distant galaxies; neutralize its heat and gravity and focus its light into a narrow beam to shine on Bethlehem only.

The point I want to make is that the Bible deals with the human spirit and the soul, the invisible world. Science is simply an organized way for us to use our God-given abilities to study the physical world and understand the mysteries of God.

If we consider that every scientific discovery is an affront to God, we do Him a great disservice.

On the scientific side, one must recognize at the onset that we deal only with the physical world, and one must not jump up and down with every new scientific discovery, declaring that God is dead.

Footprints on the Sand

It was said Darwin never denied the existence of God, even on his deathbed. While his work on evolution is a good example of scientific research, many scientists believe that it shows the orderly processes of creation, but in no way deny the existence of a creator.

A popular joke during my college days went like this:

An evolutionist named Evo was lecturing to his roommate that everything happened purely by chance.

Evo: If you take a thousand trained monkeys and put them on a thousand typewriters (no personal computers in the fifties), they will produce all the writings of Shakespeare in a thousand years.

Roommate: Come on!

Evo: Okay. Let's make it a million monkeys in a million years.

Roommate: Well, that's better. However, what happens when the monkeys die?

Evo: That's detail. The important thing is getting the concept right. Right?"

A bit of scientific trivial pursuit: Suppose the typewriter has fifty keys. Assuming that all the keys are pressed randomly and independently, and each key has an equal chance of being pressed. Now, try the phrase: "To be, or not to be," the famous phrase of Hamlet. There are twenty letters and spaces, the probability is: $(1/50^{20}) = 1/$astronomical!

($50^{20} = 9.53674 \times 10^{33}$, note that a trillion is just 10^{12}!).

Now, Shakespeare is just getting started. If you still think that Evo is right, I have a bridge on the back side of the moon to sell to you, cheap!

In medical science, most experienced physicians have encountered some unexplainable healings. Instead of calling them miracles, they name them "spontaneous remissions" and leave them at that.

In scientific research, one often encounters new observations one cannot readily explain. The first thing one does is to name it. Then we study its effects and use inductive and deductive reasoning to explore its nature further.

Gravity is a prime example. Newton named it the "force of universal attraction." He studied its effect and determined the universal gravitational constant and the law of gravitation. But what is gravity? Why does it exist? No one knows. It was speculated that if the gravitational constant changed a little, the Big Bang may have become a small bang.

A Bit of Scientific History of Gravity

The earliest writing on the subject was attributed to Aristotle (384–322 BC), a Greek philosopher. He believed that heavier objects fall faster than smaller, lighter objects.

Then came Galileo (1564–1642), an Italian mathematician and astronomer who believed gravitational accelerations are the same for heavier or lighter objects. Alas, the opposition from the followers of Aristotle was so powerful that Galileo was forced to leave the university where he taught mathematics.

Then came Kepler (1571–1630), who developed the three laws of planetary motion. He correctly predicted the planets move in elliptical orbits with the sun at one focus.

Newton came a century later (1643–1727) and refined Kepler's laws. Kepler assumed the sun was stationary and the planets revolved around it. Newton showed the sun does not occupy such a privileged position. In a binary orbit, the two objects revolved around their center of mass.

A True Story from NASA

When the Apollo 8 space capsule was returning from the moon, NASA mission control radioed: "Who's driving up there?"

"Sir Isaac Newton," was the reply.

"What?" Mission control asked.

"Sir Isaac Newton," was again the reply from Colonel Bill Anders, the command pilot. "We're in a free-fall orbit. Only Sir Isaac Newton's gravitational force is driving us."

Just when we thought we understood the effect of gravity, Einstein's relativity arrived. A popular joke went around the scientific community in the '60s was: God said, "Let Newton be," and there was light. Then the devil said, "Let Einstein be," and restored the status quo. Each new discovery leads us to further mysteries. Sometimes it takes us centuries to learn.

All true scientists should take the attitude of Newton, who saw himself as a boy playing on the seashore, diverting now and then to find a smoother pebble, a prettier shell than ordinary, whilst the great ocean of truth lay undiscovered before him.

A Newly Found Pebble: The Power Switch

Many people do not believe in God, not because they have not been told about Jesus, but because life is more convenient not to bother with God. I was that way through MIT. At that time, many Christians quoted the Bible verse: For God so loved the world that He gave His only begotten Son, that whosoever believes in Him should not perish, but has everlasting life. (John 3:16). "Just believe," they said.

Ha! It can't be that simple. I thought.

Long after I became a Christian, my three-year-old granddaughter, Amy, asked me, "Grandpa, will you turn on the TV for me?" (Someone had misplaced the remote.)

I took her to the TV and showed her the power button. I said, "Amy, read this. What does it say?"

"PO... WA." She tried to read with her newly learned phonetics. "Power," I said. "Push it."

The TV came on. She was so excited with her newfound power button; she kept turning it on and off.

With awe, I suddenly realized the complexity behind that power button.

First of all, it turns on the electricity, which comes from some remote generator from a power station someone paid millions to build. Furthermore, the stations are run by hundreds of engineers, who were taught by thousands of teachers from numerous universities. The generators were designed and built by more engineers and technicians. The materials used came from various ores and mills run by thousands. The TV programming was created by authors, screenwriters, producers, directors, and all kinds of electronic equipment run by thousands of camera operators and technicians. The list goes on.

All that complexity is incredibly available to a three-year-old by pushing a simple button. Ha! It is that simple!

So it is with God. Faith is our "power button." Once pushed, it opens our spirits to God and all he has done and will do on our behalf. Suddenly, we know the Bible becomes not just an instruction book for our mortal lives, but also for our eternal lives.

God has prepared and planned for us to have a deep relationship with him. Christ's goodness and sacrifice on our behalf made that relationship possible.

He searches for people who will simply exercise their faith and believe in him and follow His teachings. Truthfully, no one is too far from God's love. No one is too small for God's work. No sin is too great for God to forgive.

> If we confess our sins, he is faithful and just to forgive us our sins and to cleanse us from all unrighteousness.
>
> —1 John 1:9

> God did not send His Son into the world to condemn the world, but that the world through Him might be saved.
>
> —John 3:17

There's a saying that when we were born, we were given a bucket of marbles. Each day we take out a marble, and it is gone. No one knows how many marbles are left in his or her bucket. As your hair turns white, each marble becomes more precious.

I am spending this marble to share my first-hand experience with you. Most people reject God not because they know better, but because they don't understand the mystery. In Chapter 5, we talked about the miracle machine: our bodies. In Chapter 6, we discussed our wonderful minds. We either die being ignorant of God's design and plan for our lives, or we accept and learn from it. The Bible says:

> What profit is there if you gain the whole
> world and lose eternal life?
> What can be compared with the values of eternal life?
> —Matthew 16:26, the Living Bible

We're spiritual beings on an earthly journey. God is reaching his hand to you now. Take it, and you'll never walk alone into eternity.

> Today, if you hear my voice, do not harden your hearts.
> —Hebrews 4:7

Don't gamble on your eternity!

Footnote: Soon after I became a Christian, I was immediately reminded to write a letter to Mrs. Grannas, who had given me Sunday dinners and the Bible years earlier in 1951; to thank her for her kindness. Unknown to me, she was going through a tough family crisis. She thought she was a failure, and my letter encouraged her. She ultimately went on to help run an orphanage in the Philippines. What she did in her life will echo in eternity also.

Summary

We live in the two worlds, the physical world (the visible world) and the spiritual world (the invisible world). One is temporal; the other eternal.

Success is dependent on "choices" and "actions." The choices are based on the properties of the spiritual world (the invisible world), such as philosophy, faith, hope, love, ideas, determination, knowledge, wisdom, attitude, etc. When we turn good choices into actions in the physical world, we create success.

We design our successes in the invisible, spiritual world; we build them in the visible, physical world.

One prime example is the application of the success triangle of "faith, hope, and love" as opposed to the failure triangle of "fear, worry, and greed." Our choice to dwell and feed on one or the other makes all the difference.

In our physical world, we often face challenges and circumstances beyond our control, such as job loss, sickness, accidents, wars, etc. When that happens, we're pushed into the "failure triangle." Fortunately, we can seek our refuge in God and move back to the "success triangle," find our direction and get on track again.

When the storms hit, remember the sun is always shining above the atmosphere. Likewise, no matter what happens in our lives, our God is always in control. Keep this thought, and you'll have unshakable hope and learn how to dance in the rain. Before you dance in the rain, however, bring an umbrella. We must do our part. Remember when God parted the Red Sea, he didn't send a limo. We must do our part and walk across it.

We read stories about POWs and survivors from the Holocaust. Many who survived unbelievable torture and inhumane treatment found their ultimate strength in the spiritual world.

Indeed, as the psalmist said repeatedly, God is our refuge in time of need.

We're spiritual beings on an earthly journey. Our physical bodies will ebb away in time. When that happens, we go home!

Christ made it clear when he told Nicodemus in John 3:3, "Very truly I tell you. No one can see the Kingdom of God without being born again!" He went on to say, "Flesh gives birth to flesh, but the Spirit gives birth to the spirit." (John 3:6)

We live in a multidimensional world. Once we understand the relationships between these dimensions, we'll live better, more fulfilled lives by working smarter in reaching for our dreams.

Now we see through a glass darkly, but then face to face.

Summary

—1 Corinthians 13:12

Enjoy your earthly journey!

We Build a New Tomorrow

We build a new tomorrow,
We draw the pattern clear,
We make our plans with wisdom,
For God is always here.

Our thinking makes our future,
Our actions pave the way;
We build a new tomorrow,
On plans we make today!

—Dr. Arvella Schuller

Appendix A

The Amazing Hummingbird

Hummingbirds are small birds in the family **Trochilidae**. They're known for their ability to hover in midair by rapidly flapping their wings fifteen to eighteen times per second (depending on the species). Capable of sustained hovering, the hummingbird has the ability to fly deliberately backward or vertically and maintain its relative position while drinking from swaying flower blossoms. Normal flight speed is about twenty-five miles per hour. They live about four years on average. The record is seventeen.

With the exception of insects, hummingbirds, while in flight, have the highest metabolism of all animals. For some species, their heartbeats can reach as high as 1,260 beats per minute. They typically consume more than their weight in food each day. At any given moment, they're only hours away from starving. However, they are capable of slowing their metabolism at night or any time food isn't readily available. They enter a hibernation-like state and slow their heart rate to roughly 50 instead of 180 beats per minute, reducing their need for food.

The most amazing fact is that the migrating ruby-throated hummingbird can cross eight hundred kilometers (five hundred miles) of the Gulf of Mexico on a nonstop flight and lose fifty percent or more of its body weight in the process. It may look fragile, but it's truly one of the toughest creatures in the animal kingdom.

From an engineering standpoint, the hummingbird has no business flying. Its energy conversion efficiency is incredible. Its brain function, navigation, and station-keeping ability are uncanny. To have a machine that works so hard and lasts for four to seventeen years, the MTBF (mean time between failures—an engineering term in measuring reliability of a device) is unbelievable. Furthermore, it can reproduce, raise the young, and continue the species.

I'm left in awe of the capability, complexity, and intricacy built into something no bigger than my thumb! To believe that "nothing" created the hummingbird or that it came from random mutation of the genes through time requires much more faith than I have.

Appendix B

On Stress Management

Stress is a necessary part of growth, both physically and mentally. Overstressing ourselves physically will cause much pain, while the effect of overstressing mentally can be more devastating. Yet no significant human endeavor can ever be achieved without stress. The important thing is not to avoid stress, but to manage it properly.

I have learned beneficial stress management techniques through the years. These were first written in a letter to my daughter, Doreen** when she faced challenges while a freshman at the Stanford University.

She was always one of the top students in her high school and was one of the few accepted by Stanford. We were proud of her. In her first year, Doreen found that the competition was very intense. It seemed that every other student was a valedictorian from somewhere, and she was stressing out, wondering if she could fit in. Here are my advices:

1. **It's not important to be the best; it's always important to do your very best.** There's a big difference between these two. To be the best always requires effort and talent, and there are always people with more talent. To try to be the best will inevitably lead to frustration

and exhaustion. On the other hand, if you do your very best, you can take time to think, to evaluate yourself, and find how to get the best out of your God-given talent. Many people are stressed out because they're like a lemon tree that wants to grow apples or a marathon runner trying to run a four-minute mile.

2. **Don't try to bring forth fruit before its time**. Wait upon the Lord. It takes time to accomplish everything. Learn to labor and to wait. Do your best with your talent; where it leads is always in God's hands. Learn to let go and let God.

3. **Accept what life offers in stride**. Good things aren't necessarily good; bad things aren't necessarily bad. Learn the wisdom from the Chinese proverb "塞翁失馬, 焉知非福." Literally, it translates" "Mr. Tsai lost his horse. Who knew it wasn't a blessing?" (For story details, see Ref 30.)

4. **Learn a lesson from the palm tree**. Do you know why there are so many palm trees in the tropical islands? The palm tree's branches are high and reach for the sun. It gets its share of nourishment from above. Its trunk bends with the wind. In a tropical storm or hurricane, few palms are up-rooted while oak trees are much stronger, but few survive a severe storm. When the storm is over, the palm stands up again. It's a survivor! When a storm in life hits, learn to bend and hang on and keep telling yourself "This, too, shall pass." In the final analysis, above the storm, the sun always shines. God is still in control.

5. Life is like a **marathon, and we're destined to run it.** The training is vigorous, and the stress sometimes overbearing. At times you will think you cannot take it anymore. That's good! Because unless you are challenged to the limit and found wanting, you will never know your true potential and will never grow up.

The objective of running the marathon is not to win the prize, but to run it at your best pace and finish it well.

The Marathon

Twenty-six-miles, What a run.
It started hours ago.
It's now finally done!

Thousands and thousands of runners;
Only one has won.
The rest are all losers; How can it be fun?

Looking at the runners
Who stagger through the finish line,
Their bodies are full of perspiration,
But their faces are full of pride.

What fool these runners are, you say. Why work so hard from day to day?
The prize so small, the distance so long,
I'd rather be singing a song.

But look again, my friends.
They may be exhausted from the stress and strain,
But the joy in their hearts is overflowing
Because *there's no gain without pain.*

They all know a secret.
There's no need to be the best.
Winning is to let God's given talent
Have a true and supreme test.

So run, marathon runner, run!
I know you're having fun.
Those aching muscles, sweat, and tears, The discipline and training from year to year,
Have given you a sound body, spirit, and mind,
And you will stand the test of time.

So each morning when you rise,
Light up your spark of divine fire.
It does not matter if you win or lose,
To your own self, be true!

—R. C. K. Lee 2-26-84

** (My daughter graduated with honors from Stanford and received her MBA from the Wharton School of Business.)

Begin Each Day with a Proper Attitude

Start each day with "Good morning, God!" not "Good God, morning!" Begin with your devotions, thank God for your health, and reaffirm your values and goals. Write your "to do list" and ask God for guidance.

Always remember:

> The horse is prepared for the day of battle,
> but deliverance is of the Lord.
> —Proverbs 21:31

Go out each morning with your head held high and a smile on your face.

End Each Day with Thanksgiving.

A peaceful heart is a thankful heart. Regardless of the outcome of each day, thank God for his blessings and the lessons you've learned. Don't let the sun go down on your anger; learn to forgive those who might have hurt you. Harboring anger and resentment will rob you of needed rest and hurts only yourself. Learn to manage your emotions.

Commit your problems and concerns to God and have a blessed rest.

How Stress Affects Your Body

Modern research has shown that if you're stressed and "feed" yourself a steady diet of negative thoughts and emotions, you'll eventually produce massive quantities of acidic trash and waste in your body (Acidosis). This causes pH imbalance in your body. Your immune system becomes severely sluggish. Your endocrine system gets out of whack. Your vital organs begin to shut down, and your bones become brittle. If this acidic state continues, the result is chronic depression, disease, even death.

Bits of Wisdom

Bits of wisdom, consistently applied, will enhance your quality of life.

Form This Good Habit

Always sleep with a pen and pad of paper beside your bed. Your mind never sleeps. Sometimes your best inspirations, ideas, and solutions come in the middle of the night when you're suddenly awakened from a sound sleep. By the way, a voice recorder works even better.

Tips on Driving

1. If you rent a car, find a credit card that offers full supplemental collision insurance. It's expensive to buy it from the rental companies.

2. When parking in a garage, always park with the driver's side facing uphill. Reason: 95 percent of cars in the United States are driven by a single driver. You're much less likely to be banged by other car doors as a result of gravity.

3. When parking in a mall, pull forward to the space in front when possible so you can drive forward when you leave. Reason: 95 percent of parking lot accidents happen while backing up from a parking space. In fact, it was reported some teenage gangs in Los Angeles were targeting women and elderly ladies talking on cell phones while exiting the mall. The gang members pulled quickly behind them and claimed personal injury when the accident occurred. Worse still, they got the driver's address and license (potential ID theft and robbery).

4. Don't forget the panic button on your car keys. Every modern car is equipped with one. The loud noise may save your life. Remember, you can use that at home as well. It may frighten away an intruder and summon help.

5. Don't be "an accident waiting to happen." Many young people are impatient, cutting in and out of traffic to save time. On a twenty-five-mile trip, averaging fifty miles per hour, you'll get to your destination in thirty minutes. To gain five minutes, you need to average sixty miles per hour in a fifty-mile-per-hour traffic, almost an impossible task. In the meantime, you're risking an accident each time you cut in and out. In like manner, never try to beat the red light. Many major accidents happen this way. Learn to manage your time better. Leave five minutes early.

The Safest Lane on the Freeways

According to the highway patrol, the safest lane to drive in is the lane next to the fast lane on the left (usually the third lane on the left). Reason: The two right lanes are slow lanes, full of big trucks. They are not allowed to drive in the other lanes. They often rear-end cars because they can't stop as easily as cars. The only thing worse is being sandwiched between two eighteen-wheelers. Most accidents occur in the two slow lanes. The fast lanes are the favorites for teenagers and impatient tailgaters.

Cell Phones Cause More Accidents than Drunk Driving!

The reason is people try to dial or text while driving. If you must use the cell phone, use hands-free, "dial by voice" phones or a headphone to minimize distraction.

Never text while driving!

Miscellaneous Tips and Tricks

Good nutrition in the morning

Many seniors and executives rush from the house without proper morning nutrition and suffer constipation and lack of energy.

Here's a tip from health professionals that works for me. Each morning, start it well with a blended fruit drink.

> Two cups of water
> 1/3 of an avocado
> ¼ cup of blueberries
> Small amount of three different fruits (frozen okay)
> A scoop or two of organic soybean, hemp protein, or green powder
> Couple tablespoons of psyllium husks (fiber)

Mix well in a blender. Finish with a glass of water.

This will give you most of your daily requirements of fruit, fiber, and protein. It helps keep your cholesterol under control.

If you have trouble with constipation, you'll have a good movement in thirty minutes or less.

If you want to try this, all the ingredients can be obtained from your local Trader Joe's store. (This is for your convenience; I get no commission for this.)

Caution: I do not claim to be nutritionist; I only share what works for me.

Fire and Carbon Monoxide Alarm

Check your fire and carbon monoxide alarm periodically. Replace the batteries as needed. It will save you and your family's lives. In case of fire, remember to teach your family to lie on the floor and crawl out. Smoke and heat always rise.

Pinning Your Socks

Most people spend a lot of time matching their socks after they've been laundered. Here's a simple trick: Use a safety pin to lock the pair together before the laundry. The socks will go through the washer and dryer without any problems, and you never have to sort them again.

Correct Use of the Toilet Seat Cover

Everyone knows how to use the toilet seat cover, right? Surprisingly, 95 percent don't know how to use it properly. Don't believe me? Try this test: Toilet seat covers have two sides, a shiny side and a dull side. Which side faces the seat? Here are some interesting findings. About 40 percent of the people polled chose one or the other; about 20 percent never knew the difference.

The original seat cover was designed to have the shiny side impregnated with wax to prevent wetness and some mild germicides to keep the germs from you. So if you want to use it properly, the shiny side should face the seat.

Here's what 95 percent of the people don't know: Where do you put the tongue on the toilet seat cover? The correct way is to flip it forward and cover the front of the commode. Your pants and skirts have been polishing the front of the dirty commode, usually full of germs, long enough.

Some people commented that this subject may not be appropriate for this book. Parents should teach this to their children.

"Did you know it?" I asked them. The answer was no. Well, I'm teaching parents now. (Many people actually have thanked me for this simple tip.)

Appendix C

Marriage Saver

The Perfect Mate

Joe was active in high school sports and popular with the girls. However, Joe thought he could do much better than marrying the local girls, so he set out to look for the perfect woman. Twenty years later, he returned home a dejected bachelor. Many of his friends asked him if he ever found the perfect woman. His answer was, "Yes, I found one."

"Why didn't you marry her?"

The answer, "She was looking for the perfect man!"

There is no perfect man or woman. The real question is how to make the marriage work for imperfect people.

Marriage in Four Phases

I remember watching a Chinese cartoon depicting marriage in four phases, from the woman's viewpoint

Phase 1: Young couple getting married; she calls him "honey." (爱人 ài rén) He can do no wrong. They stick together like glue.

Phase 2: Woman holding a baby surrounded by her other children; she calls her husband "Daddy." (孩子的爸爸 hái zi de bà bà).

Phase 3: Old couple arguing; she calls him (老不死 lǎo bù sǐ) "Old not dead."

Phase 4: Cemetery with a cross. The widow says, "He wasn't too bad. I miss him." (不太坏, 我想他 bù tài huài, wǒ xiǎng tā)

While this cartoon was meant to be humorous, there's a lot of truth in it. In the world, marriage should be the most blessed at phase two. Yet it's also the most vulnerable.

Why? The woman is too occupied with the children and their activities, while the man is enjoying some professional success and looks good to many lonely women, especially those at work.

Some people may think that phase three is overdramatic. When one gets old, the children are gone, physical attraction is gone, and sex is gone. Many women believe marriage is for better or worse, but not for lunch. They both have no place to go. As divorce is out of the question, they magnify each other's fault and argue!

In our observations, we saw countless well-dressed, old couples, sitting across from one another in restaurants and scarcely saying a word to each other. When they do, they were often unfriendly.

Phase four is almost universally true. Why? When one is gone, the one left will remember the sum total of the values the other had provided. The memories are sweet.

In what follows, we'll analyze the importance of providing value for one another (See Chapter 2.) and avoid problems. We'll concentrate on phase two. Most divorces happen there. If it's not fixed then, there will be no other phases.

Most Marriage Problems Started Small

John graduated from college six years ago and married Jane, his college sweetheart. They had four-year-old twin boys. Life was good when he left for his job as a supervisor of sales in his company.

By midmorning, John received the shocking news that his good friend and schoolmate, George, supervisor of customer service, was promoted to a VP position. After congratulating George, he returned to his office extremely upset. He thought he was the better man and should have gotten the job. Problems piled up in the office, and he was upset with some of his salesmen. He couldn't wait for 5:00 p.m. so he could go home and relax.

In the meantime, Jane had constant problems with the twins. They managed to stop up the toilet and make a mess of the bathroom and themselves. After she cleaned them up, they fought constantly, blaming each other. They took ice cream from the freezer and left the freezer door open. The ice cream melted on the kitchen floor. Jane was upset and warned them, "Just wait until Daddy comes home!"

When John clicked the garage door open, the twins hid. Jane greeted him with uncombed hair and told him all of her problems.

Instead of finding comfort, the "garbage dumping" drove John back to his car and into a local bar where lonely women waited to give him comfort.

In the meantime, Jane was devastated. She packed up the kids and went home to Mama.

This is often how divorce happens to a good couple. When facing stress, they magnify each other's faults until they become monsters. This is called the "divorce syndrome." It destroys many good marriages and creates tragic consequences physically, financially, and emotionally for the couple and their children.

No man grew up looking for a woman to support for life. No woman looked for a man she could cook for and take care of for life. Each was looking for someone who could provide value so together they could create a perfect union and build a perfect family.

Unfortunately, there is no perfect man or woman; each comes with his/her share of virtues and faults.

To build and preserve a good marriage, remember this: The grass you watered is always greener! So try to water each other by: (1) providing value to each other, (2) communicating and sharing your dreams and problems, and (3) breaking your big problems into small ones and working together to solve them.

Appendix C

Helpful Tools

1. The Marriage Saver To-Do List. Use this form to communicate instead of nagging each other.

2. The two signs shown below are meant to be printed on mirrors to see one's self and placed on the two sides of the entry door where to be easily seen and serve as reminders.

Marriage Saver Tools

Understanding is achieved through mutual respect of each other's priorities. Harmony is obtained through communication.

The secret of a good marriage is maintaining good communication.

MY TO-DO LIST		HONEY, PLEASE HELP ME	

LOVE beareth all things, believeth all things, and hopeth all things.
—1 Corinthians 13:7

Marriage Saver Tools

God Bless Our Happy Home.

Smile!

**Leave Your Burden Here.
Bring Only Happiness In.**

This sign is designed to be posted on a mirror and attached to the front entrance of the garage.

God Bless Our Happy Home

Treasure Your Mate.
No Garbage Dumping!

This sign is designed to be posted on a mirror and attached to the inside door to the garage.

Appendix D

Recommended Reading List

Financial:

1. The Richest Man in Babylon by George S. Clason
2. Think and Grow Rich by Napoleon Hill
3. Rich Dad, Poor Dad by Robert Kiyosaki
4. Business School by Robert Kiyosaki
5. We Want You To Be Rich by Robert Kiyosaki and Donald Trump

Motivational:

6. Built to Last by James Collins & Jerry Porras
7. The Slight Edge by Jeff Olson
8. The Road Ahead by Bill Gates
9. The Power of Positive Thinking by Dr. Norman V. Peale
10. Move Ahead with Possibility Thinking by Dr. Robert H. Schuller
11. Tough Times Never Last, Tough People Do! by Dr. Robert H. Schuller
12. My Journey by Dr. Robert H. Schuller
13. Timing Is Everything by Denis Waitley
14. See You at the Top by Zig Ziglar
15. *Man's Search for Meaning* by Viktor E. Frankl

16. Challenge to Succeed by Jim Rohn
17. Unlimited Power by Anthony Robbins

Spiritual:

18. Purpose Driven Life by Rick Warren
19. The Language of God by Dr. Francis S. Collins
20. Your Best Life Now by Joel Osteen
21. Mere Christianity by C. S. Lewis
22. The Case for Christ by Lee Strobel
23. Confidence in the Bible by Harold J. Sala
24. The Dream Giver by Bruce Wilkinson
25. Holy Discontent by Bill Hybels

Health and Miscellaneous:

26. The Enzyme Factor by Dr. Hiromi Shinya
27. The Rejuvenation Enzyme by Dr. Hiromi Shinya
28. The No Sweat Exercise Plan by Dr. Harvey B. Simon, M.D.
29. Wu and the Golden Stallion by Dr. R.C.K. Lee & Doreen Ong
30. The Art of War by Sun Tze
31. The Enlightened Prince by Dr. R.C.K. Lee & Doreen Ong
32. Temujin – the Young Worrier by Dr. R.C.K. Lee & Doreen Ong

These books are available at your local library. Each author has also written multiple books. Many books are also available in audio CDs for your drive-time education. In short, there is no end of good books for your own research.

Appendix E

Pesticides and Babies

Many pregnant women go out of their ways to eat a lot of vegetables and fruits, thinking that it will keep them and their babies healthy. Unknowingly, they consumed a lot of pesticides also as a result. These pesticides in their blood stream may not affect the mother personally at 100+ pounds, but the same blood is feeding your baby! At 9 weeks, your baby is fully formed, it weighs just 1 ounce!

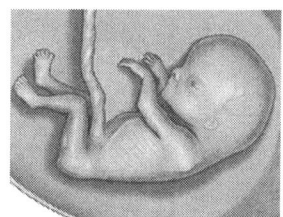

That's why it is important to clean your vegetables and fruits and remove these pesticides before eating them. As these pesticides are oil-based, one needs to use strong detergents to remove them.

Fortunately, strong Kangen Water, pH 11.5 can do the job without using chemicals. See Kangen water Demo – https://www.youtube.com/watch?v=I-bxXzCYVXU&feature=player_detailpage

Don't take my word for it, just read the research articles below:

The pediatricians at the American Academy of Pediatrics point to science linking pesticide exposure with a range of childhood health harms, from reduced birth weight to ADHD to impaired mental development.

Undermining the next generation

The second report, A Generation in Jeopardy: How pesticides are undermining our children's health & intelligence, is from our team here at Pesticide Action Network. Our scientists reviewed more than 200 recent studies exploring how pesticides are linked to a range of childhood health harms. We also took a careful look at government data tracking the trends in these diseases and disorders.

We found that today's children are less healthy than they were a generation ago, and science shows that pesticides are contributing to the trend. As a mom, I find this deeply disturbing. As public health experts are raising the alarm about a "silent pandemic" of learning disabilities and disorders, the science linking neurotoxic pesticides to harm of the developing brain grows stronger and stronger.

A few other key findings:

- 400,000 to 600,000 of the 4 million U.S. children born each year are affected by some kind of developmental disability — a 17% rise in the past 15 years. Many studies link exposure to pesticides — even at very low levels — with increased risk of ADHD, autism and falling IQs.

Appendix E

- Incidence of leukemia and childhood brain tumors, now the two most common types of childhood cancer, have risen 40% and 50%, respectively since 1975. Studies suggest that pesticides are contributing to this trend.

- Today, more than 7 million U.S. children are affected by asthma, up from 2 million in 1980. Emerging science points to pesticides as a possible contributing factor.

Pesticides are certainly not the *only* driver of these health harms. Scientists agree there are many factors at play, and that there is often a combination of genetics and environmental contaminants involved.

<u>But pesticide exposure is a piece of the puzzle that we can do something about.</u>

You can find loads more info. from Google.

Author's Biography

Dr. Robert C. K. Lee

Dr. Lee is an eighty-four year old retired rocket scientist who has worked on the Gemini program, Titan II & III launch vehicles and several satellite projects. He has received a "Special Achievement Award" from the USAF Space Division. He earned his BS, MS, and Ph.D. degrees from MIT.

He also taught as a tenured professor at the University of California at Irvine (UCI). He is the author of *Optimal Estimation, Identification, and Control*, MIT Press, and also published in numerous technical papers and articles. Dr. Lee holds many patents ranging from the area of missiles and aircraft to recreational vehicles. He was listed in *Who's Who in the West* in 1970–1971.

Dr. Lee is also active in the business. He owned and operated several small businesses and franchises in his youth. In management, he has served as chairman and CEO of a commuter airline, vice-chairman of a national bank, and chairman and president of several companies. He was elected as "Entrepreneur of the Year 2004" by ABAOC.

Dr. Lee recently retired as chairman of the China International University Foundation (CIUF), a 501 (c)(3) corporation. The main purpose of this foundation is to improve understanding between the East and West and to promote world peace. The motto of this university is "Putting wings in young hearts."

He also authored "Beat Your Opponent" – An instructional book on playing bridge. He also co-authored the Chinese Treasure Chest Series of children's books with his daughter, Doreen. The authors believe that you build smart kids by teaching them early to "think outside the box". These stories are like the oriental Aesop's fables and are available at Amazon.com and www.dragonwisdompress.com.

Dr. Lee is active in Christian and community service. He served many years as an elder of the Crystal Cathedral. He and his wife, Bettie, were members of the UCI Chancellor's Club and the UCI Chao Family Comprehensive Cancer Center Support Group.

***** Five Star Book Reviews *****

Dr. Lee is a retired professor of Engineering as well as an entrepreneur in business. His study and practice of his philosophy, including Christian and community service made great advances in the connection of Eastern and Western wisdom and compassion. This book is very unique. It is highly recommended.

> Dr. H. Yeh, Professor of Engineering

Congratulations, Dr. Lee, for a job well done. You are leaving your legacy to the next generation by writing this book and sharing all the success stories and the wisdom of a Chinese scholar. I am so touched. I recommend this book to all my friends and their off- springs…

> Dr. Danni Sun – Business entrepreneur

God has a unique purpose for each one of His children. This book will inspire the readers to live up to his/her God given dreams and potentials. The inspiring stories of famous persons will help people to make a difference in the world.

> Mary Lee Ehrlich – Christian author

I found this book to be most interesting and motivating. The readers will benefit greatly from the author's experience and wisdom. I particularly enjoyed the juxtaposition of Eastern and Western examples and anecdotes.

T. F Meier – CEO, Pro-"**M**" **Systems**

There were many wise insights in the book. I believe that this is more of a motivation book than a how-to book. It certainly lifted my spirits as a valued human being and offers some suggested direction for life. It is also a book on how not to fail by abusing substances. I found this book very useful for myself and I believe it will be very useful to many others.

H. Chen, CEO, WorldTech Devices.

This book should be required readings for all high school and college graduates.

R. Ding – Philanthropist

As an independent businessman, I found this book to be both meaningful and practical. It offers insights to all about how to deal with the rough but rewarding roads ahead and overcome obstacles with the applied wisdom from the East and the West. He uses the stories of famous people as well as his own personal experience to show how to overcome frustrations and set- backs on the roads to success. He teaches you how to enjoy the sunshine and also dance in the rain!

J. Clover, Independent Businessman

***** Five Star Book Reviews *****

Your blending of the Eastern & Western cultures is spellbinding because your stories haven't been told over here in the West and they hold our attention as you make your points with ancient wisdom in today's modern world.

As the President of Future Foundation Wellness, I especially enjoyed Chapter 5: "Our Vibrant Health" as not many people get the pleasure of reading such an enjoyable book written by a prominent, rocket scientist, especially one that covers not just the physical, but also the mental and spiritual realm as well.

Your accomplishments deserve to have you listed in "Who's Who" in the world of exceptional people and we're proud to know you.

M. Kinnett, President – Future Foundation Water Inc.

I have known Dr. Lee for decades, both as a friend and business partner. I know first-hand about his character, dedication and integrity. His devotion to his mission of helping people is exemplary. This book's message will help a lot of young people on their road to building health and wealth. His use of the rainbow to represent the seven areas of self-development is unique and helpful. I highly recommend this book.

D. Dimacale, Entrepreneur and Businessman

"Dr. Lee, Your book is a treasure chest of valuable information and a must read for all people in pursuit of optimal health, prosperity, and harmony in their lives."

Louis Petrossi
Founder -President
The Wealth Research Institute

Index

Acid reflux, 171

Acidosis, 152

Aerospace Corp, 266

Albert Einstein, 189, 237, 240, 274

Alcohol, 159, 164

American Cancer Society, 164

Aristotle, 63, 69, 134

Bill Gates, 8, 80, 101, 278

Blaise Pascal, 238

Brain, 156

Breast cancer, 156

C.S. Lewis, 243, 310

Cancer, 150

Confucius, 16, 20

Crystal Cathedral, 96, 196, 206, 267

Dancing in the rain, 261

Disney Company, 74

Don Quixote, 52

DOS, 9

Evolution, 234

Faith, 62

Fantasia, 74, 206

Food Abuse, 168 – 171

Footprints on the Sand, 233, 243

Forest Lanes, 78

Galileo, 238, 275, 278

Gandhi, 36

Greed, 80

Gregor Mendel, 239

Helen Keller, viii

Hope, 62, 75, 78

Hour of Power, 91, 197

How to Live Long, 175

Hummingbird, 253, 287

Jesus Christ, 67, 228

Johannes Kepler, 237

Kangen Water, 126, 158, 270

Kon-Ming, 69

Louis Pasteur, 239

Love, 62, 79, 80

Marriage, 44, 299

Mary Poppins, 103

Mary Stevenson, 245

Mastermind Principle, 191

Max Planck, 152

Metastasis, 151

Michael Faraday, 239

Microsoft, 8, 106

MISS Project, 265

Move Ahead with Possibility Thinking, 267, 309

Mrs. Grannas, 251, 282

Nicholas Copernicus, 239

Obesity, 168, 273

Optimal Estimation, Identification and control, 265

Ostfriesland, 10

Penicillin, 30, 31

Phagocytes, 145

Platelets, 269

Prayer of Thanksgiving, 265

Princeton University, 2

Qing Dynasty, 21

Red blood cells, 142

Rene Descartes, 238

Reproduction Paradox, 136

Rick Warren, 243

Robert Boyle, 239

Robert Frost, iv

Robert H Schuller, 206

Ryan's Well, 12

Secrets of Staying in Love, 196

Sexual Abuse, 167

Sir Francis Bacon, 238

Sir Isaac Newton, 237

Sleep apnea, 171

Stress Management, 289

Success Triangle, 58

Tang Dynasty, 223

Thomas Bayes, 237

Tobacco, 161

Tze Lu, 16

Valley Forge, 81

Water Can, 13

Wernher Von Braun, 240

White Blood Cells, 142, 176

William Thomson, 239

William Wu, 252

Worry, 75

X-15 Space Plane, 263

Xerox, 102

Yang, 44, 194

Yin, 44, 194

Made in the USA
San Bernardino, CA
12 January 2017